Extraordinary Acclaim for Eliana Gil's

Outgrowing the Pain:
A Book for and About Adults Abused as Children

"ANYONE WHO HAD A TROUBLED CHILDHOOD OUGHT TO READ THIS BOOK."
> —Anne H. Cohn, D.P.H., Executive Director, National Committee for Prevention of Child Abuse

"THE BEST BOOK AVAILABLE TO HELP SURVIVORS COPE AND UNDERSTAND."
> —Dan Sexton, Director, Childhelp's National Child Abuse Hotline

"READABLE. . . . It's a good introduction—or supplement—for people working on issues of anger and codependency, for adult children of alcoholics and people who love too much."
> —Portland *Oregonian*

"*OUTGROWING THE PAIN* exposes self-defeating tendencies and shows how different and more positive patterns may be developed . . . an essential tool in coping with child abuse . . . should not be missed."
> —*The Midwest Book Review*

"AN INVALUABLE AID for adult survivors of child abuse."
> —Suzanne M. Sgroi, M.D., Executive Director, New England Clinical Associates

Outgrowing the Pain Together

Also by Eliana Gil

Outgrowing the Pain: A Book for and About Adults Abused as Children

Outgrowing the Pain Together:

A Book for Spouses and Partners of Adults Abused as Children

Eliana Gil, Ph.D.

A DELL TRADE PAPERBACK

A DELL TRADE PAPERBACK
Published by
Dell Publishing
a division of
Bantam Doubleday Dell Publishing Group, Inc.
1540 Broadway
New York, New York 10036

Illustrations by Sally Haskell

The trademark Dell® is registered in the U.S. Patent and Trademark Office.

ISBN: 0-440-50372-8

Printed in the United States of America

Published simultaneously in Canada

July 1992

10   9   8   7

BVG

I'd like to thank Jody Rein for her encouragement to write this book. Also, my editor Trish Todd helped crystallize my ideas and shared her enthusiasm for this project. My gratitude to my husband and family and friends for supporting me through my often chaotic and demanding work schedule. And finally, my appreciation to the survivors and their spouses and partners who have shared and trusted and who struggle to strengthen and enhance their relationships.

To my partner for life,
with love

Contents

Why Should I Read This Book?

This book is written for partners, friends, and spouses of adult survivors of childhood abuse. Those of you who love survivors know that it can be difficult to establish and then maintain intimate relationships. You may find yourself wondering if things will ever work out, if your partner will ever "get over" his or her childhood abuse, if you will ever have a "normal" relationship. You may have experienced a number of feelings that worry or trouble you—fear, distrust, impatience, lack of communication, anger, sadness, compassion, and hope for the future are but a few. These feelings may scare you, confuse you, or make you feel helpless. You may feel like leaving the relationship out of sheer frustration and despair. If you have a relationship with an adult survivor of childhood abuse, you will need some support and guidance of your very own.

Survivors can make wonderful friends, lovers, and companions. Getting these relationships off the ground, and keeping crises to a minimum, can be quite challenging. Understanding the adult survivor of childhood abuse is the first step.

If you are a survivor yourself, it will be important for you to understand how your own issues may create additional difficulty. Be sure you have given your own needs as a survivor sufficient attention.

Don't hesitate to seek out mental health professionals to consult if difficulties in the relationship persist or grow more severe over time.

If your survivor/partner is unwilling to undergo therapy, you can still receive valuable assistance for yourself that can benefit your relationship.

Introduction

When children are physically abused in their families, they learn a very strong lesson: People who love you hurt you. They experience the abuse in the context of a (supposedly) loving relationship, so already there is some confusion. This is further complicated by the fact that children are dependent on parents or caretakers for their very survival, and children naturally long to be loved and nurtured by parental figures.

When the parents, caretakers, or siblings alternately nurture and then hurt the child, the natural outcome is that the abused child begins to associate love with pain, as if one is always followed by the other.

I once worked with an abused girl of six. She came to counseling sessions for four months, at which time she brought me a paddle. "What's this?" I asked. "It's a paddle," she responded quickly. "And what's it for?" I inquired. "It's for you to hit me," she said matter-of-factly. Alarmed, I asked, "Why would I want to hit you?" and she quietly said, "You like me, don't you?" It was clear that since she felt I liked her, the next thing she envisioned was that I would hit her. She even provided the weapon, not because she liked being hit, but because she was certain that the hitting would be part of our relationship, and she wanted to make it easier for me. Some people get confused by this kind of "reasoning." They speculate that the child enjoys being hit. Nothing could be further from the truth. In this little girl's mind, getting hit was the price she paid for positive attention.

Children who are sexually abused learn a different lesson: People who love you are sexual with you. Sexually abused children learn to associate love with sexuality, and expect that others want only sexual contact from them. Sexually abused children can have many reactions to the abuse; physical abuse is a little more clear-cut because there is physical pain. Sexual abuse can feel good and bad at the same time. It can be the only time that children receive affection or warmth, but at the same time, children may feel frightened and scared. As they mature and learn about sexuality, a variety of responses can occur. Sexual contact may be avoided, since it is viewed as a frightening or unpleasant experience. Conversely, an individual can have numerous sexual encounters and yet may not want or enjoy sex, and does not view it as a way to feel close, warm, or intimate. Instead, sexuality may be viewed as a way to be safe, in control, or as a price to be paid for attention or affection. Adults who were sexually abused as children may eventually want to be sexually active with a chosen, trusted partner, and yet he or she may find it virtually impossible to relax, enjoy, or have physical or emotional feelings during sexual contact. Flashbacks of the abuse may interrupt lovemaking, causing self-doubts, guilt, and fear in both parties.

These and other potential problems can be overcome! Adult survivors can enjoy full and active sexual lives as long as the obstacles are identified and prevention plans are carefully developed. (The other key factor is the presence of a patient, loving, committed friend or partner, willing to understand the impact of childhood abuse and wanting to work with the survivor toward the mutual goal of building a healthy and loving relationship.)

Children who are neglected expect to be ignored or abandoned. They lived with parents who were withholding or uninterested, and who failed to provide physical affection, guidance, support, encouragement, or positive feedback. Neglected children seem to long for human contact, and yet may be uncertain about how to ask for (or accept) positive attention. As adults, individuals who were neglected may shy away from relationships. They may be very isolated, avoiding the contact they long for the most. They have been disappointed frequently, and they may feel afraid to risk disappointment again. For survivors, trust will develop very slowly, and once it does the neglected adult may suddenly express a range of unmet needs, overwhelming the partner with expressed or implied requests.

Finally, emotional abuse is also devastating to children. Emotionally abusive parents can be alternately withholding and attacking. They verbally assault the child with critical, judgmental, harsh and hurtful statements. Very young children cannot defend against this abuse because they don't have an established sense of who they are; children get their

Partners may feel overwhelmed with expressed or implied requests.

sense of self from parents and caretakers who give them messages about their strengths, talents, and special qualities. If the only messages are negative, the child is unable to develop positive regard. If neither positive nor negative attention is given, the child can feel undefined and vague. Adults with a history of emotional abuse perceive relationships as impossible to obtain for themselves. They believe they have nothing to offer, and that others will not care what they think or feel. They isolate themselves and lead emotionally empty lives. In addition, the messages once given by abusive parents are now incorporated by the adult survivors, who constantly repeat the negative statements to themselves. Survivors tell me that they hear voices in their heads repeating phrases such as "You're so stupid," "People will laugh if you say that," or "You're ugly and fat." Given this negative and harsh view of themselves, survivors of emotional abuse don't usually seek out relationships with others. They feel inferior and unworthy of positive attention.

Lessons learned in childhood serve as the foundation for adult relationships. Children learn from parents and caretakers about love, affection, intimacy, sexuality, morality, trust, dependency, communication, and expression of feelings. Adult survivors shaped their attitudes, behaviors, and thoughts by observing their parents and caretakers. These lessons are mentally stored in childhood and emerge in adulthood. This does not mean that people are doomed to repeat unhealthful patterns of relating, but it does mean that those adults whose childhood experiences included physical, emotional, or sexual abuse and neglect must work pretty hard on establishing and enhancing healthy relationships. A history of abuse almost always means hard work to overcome obstacles. Having a history of abuse can contribute to certain problems, but if the problems are anticipated, and steps taken to resolve them, prevention efforts can really pay off.

A history of abuse also means taking chances. Survivors

must seek out contact with others who are safe and trustworthy, establish a support network, and create a safe environment where new behaviors can be tested.

Imagine that someone is asked to walk along an open field, and quickly discovers that there are many dangerous swamps and pits. Any movement is risky. The pits are hidden and the swamps seem to appear suddenly. Now imagine that this person is given a map of the area, and the pits and swamps are clearly marked. Now the person can make plans to avoid the pitfalls and get to his or her destination unharmed.

Now the person can make plans to avoid pitfalls.

The adult survivor is not the only one who needs to antici-pate and plan for problem situations. Those who care about and have relationships with adult survivors can also gain a better understanding of where the obstacles may be, and how to respond appropriately. Relationships with adult survivors require effort, and they can be extremely rewarding. The efforts are an investment that will definitely pay off. Adult survivors have waited a long time to feel safe, loved, and secure. They have also waited a lifetime to share their love, warmth, joy, and affection with someone else.

Chapter 1

ANGER

Sailing Through Uncharted Waters

I'm damned if I do and damned if I don't. If I let off a little steam, she acts as if I've just beaten her up and she won't talk to me for weeks. If I keep it to myself, she accuses me of not trusting her and she threatens to leave. No matter what I do, I end up feeling like the bad guy and she ends up treating me like I'm the guy who used to shove his fist down her throat.

Anger is **just another feeling.** Right? *Wrong.* To adult survivors, anger is one of the most frightening, confusing, paralyzing, and uncomfortable of feelings.

Adult survivors of physical abuse grew up in environments where anger was expressed in uncontrolled, violent ways. Anger was seen as threatening and powerful.

Here is a typical scenario. Jamie comes home from school feeling anxious. She doesn't know why she's scared, but she notices that as she gets two or three blocks from home her stomach hurts, her muscles get tense, and she doesn't breathe as easily. As she gets to the door she listens. She gets equally upset if it's too quiet or if loud screams are heard. She walks in slowly, cautiously looking around. She finds her father and immediately smells the alcohol. Her body gets more constricted, and all she can think of is how to get quietly to her room without being noticed. Sometimes she succeeds and tries to become invisible in her room, forgoing dinner or TV watching and crawling under the covers early in the evening. Other times she's not as lucky and her very presence provokes an angry attack. She's never sure what she will do to set it off—one day it was the way she wore her hair down, "like a slut"; another day it was the way she wore her hair up, like an "uptight bitch." It seemed if she looked away, she would get hit, yet if she looked at her father, this could get him more upset. If tears were seen by her father, she would be dragged to the bathroom, where her face would be pushed in the toilet. If no tears came, her father thought she was being "sassy."

This child has no options. She is attacked for what she does and what she doesn't do. It appears her very being provokes an assault. She must develop defenses, and one of the best is physical and emotional paralysis. Another is to flee emotionally.

Just as powerful as actual physical attacks and the inconsistency in which they happen is the **threat of harm** without the actual physical abuse. Your spouse or partner might have grown up in an environment where paddles, bats, or belts were frequently taken out and shown to the child, accompanied by the foreboding message "You better obey, or else. . . ." These children also live with anxiety and fear, and may develop a variety of coping skills to tolerate this threatening and potentially unsafe environment. It's possible in these families that no direct harm is done to the child, but the family pet is beaten or kicked or burned in front of the child. You can imagine the child's response to witnessing a loved pet get hurt and then being told that he or she will be next!

The child will naturally regard anger as a frightening and potentially violent emotion.

Another destructive situation is to live in a home where the children are not physically hurt, yet the adults are frequently explosive and brutal with each other. The children watch motionless, powerless to rescue the victim or stop the aggressor.

The children watch the aggressor motionless.

For the child witness of parental violence, guilt, fear, and desperation are felt and yet ambivalence is usually present as well, because children love and depend on the adults they are watching.

There are a couple of other ways in which families can confuse or frighten children about the emotion of anger. One is the family that uses words violently; the impact of emotional abuse cannot be underestimated. When a parent assaults a child with critical and demeaning comments, the child takes them in, eventually believing them to be true. Long after an emotionally abusive parent has stopped using the abusive phrases, the child hears the words internally. The parent's words are powerful because children get a sense of who they are and what they are worth from their parents. Parents are the most significant teachers a child has because children totally trust and depend on them.

Emotionally and verbally abused children learn that anger is a way to launch negative assaults that can be precipitated by a specific event or can occur without any visible provocation.

Your partner or spouse may have been raised in a family where anger was not an acceptable emotion, and the lesson taught was "keep it to yourself." These are families in which the anger is swallowed and expression of anger is not allowed or encouraged. Individuals who do not have permission to express anger may find any sign of anger unacceptable or frightening, and may wish to retreat and withdraw at the slightest hint of conflict.

Lastly, it is possible that your partner may have identified with the aggressor, and may have learned the lessons of the parent too well. These adults express anger the way they saw it expressed when they were children. They may say to themselves, "Nobody's ever gonna intimidate me again," and they proceed to attack before anyone dares attack them.

Anger is not a comfortable emotion to most people; to

people who grew up in physically or emotionally abusive families, it can feel like an insurmountable problem. Although each person in a relationship will have angry feelings at one time or another, what becomes critical is to have specific safe and appropriate ways of expressing anger and to create an environment in which anger is treated as **just another feeling**, a feeling to be understood, acknowledged, and expressed. Here are some suggestions for creating such an environment:

- Talk about anger
- Try to understand your partner's experience of anger
- Tell each other what each of you would like regarding anger
- Practice when you're not angry
- Define high-risk situations and trigger words
- Talk about out-of-control anger
- Create nonverbal signals and alternatives
- Never let anger build up (like steam in a kettle)
- Use your body to release anger
- Express anger in safe ways

Talk About Anger

For adult survivors, the emotion of anger can be troubling, confusing, and problematic. Negative associations between anger and frightening feelings have been made. It is likely that survivors were never encouraged or allowed to have or show angry feelings. It is also possible that many childhood experiences involving the expression of anger have been forgotten or pushed away. There may be many unresolved feelings from childhood.

Being in an intimate relationship, or creating a family environment, may bring back some of these memories at unexpected moments. One adult survivor told me she was shocked to learn that she expected her husband to hit her when she made a mistake. She did not believe in violence, and did not want violence to be part of her life, yet very soon after the wedding she found herself reacting to her husband in ways she remembered her mother reacting to her abusive father. Being married, and dealing with the normal problems of intimacy, elicited memories of her own childhood. In order to understand her reactions, she first had to make the link to her childhood experiences.

Talking about anger is a useful thing to do; it takes the mystery out of this emotion. It gives people the opportunity to (1) understand the lessons they have learned in childhood, and (2) think about and plan how they want to express angry feelings in the future. I will now make a few suggestions for talking about anger, and recommend an exercise for you to try. As I emphasize throughout this book, you can never change anyone else, or control anyone else. The following suggestions are made for you. You can try them alone or with a friend. If your partner or spouse is willing and able to do these exercises with you, that's great.

Begin this exercise, "Thinking and Talking About Anger," by telling yourself, or your friend or spouse, what you are doing. Make a simple statement, such as "I've decided it's important for me to think about anger in my life.". . . "How you show anger is something that's learned in life, and I am going to think about what lessons I learned about anger as I grew up." If you are sharing with someone else, it might be useful to make a list of your thoughts and memories prior to sharing.

Now think about (and describe) the ways in which each of your parents and/or siblings used to show anger. Think about ways of expressing anger that were rewarded and ways of expressing anger that were punished. Think about times when either of your parents expressed anger in ways they later apologized for. Notice any discrepancies between what you were told to do and not do, and how others behaved. (Even though parents frequently insist that children not, for

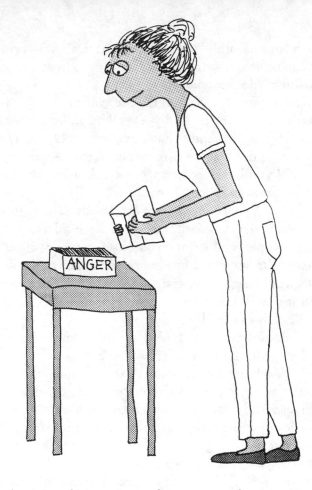

example, raise their voices when angry, they may set that example by yelling at kids when they are upset.)

Also, think about any experiences at home involving the expression of anger that were unusual or significant. Some children remember a single event that precipitated a major outburst on the part of a parent. If so, think about how people in the family reacted to that single event. Some adults are able to recall that things around home were pretty peaceful except during specific times, like the holidays or when extended family members visited. Still others remember that things went smoothly unless Mom or Dad was drinking. Adults may characterize their drinking parents as having Jekyll and Hyde personalities.

Consider your reactions to the various ways people showed you their anger. Did you yell back, leave the house, get sick, eat a lot, or simply stay out of sight? Did you forgive and forget, or did you feel anxious until the next time? What lessons did you learn about anger as a child in your family? See if you can write them down.

Once you've envisioned how your family dealt with anger, contemplate the lessons learned at school, from your teachers and peers. What memories do you have about how people (adults and children) expressed anger at school? Do any teachers, coaches, ministers, or other adults in position of authority stand out? How did they deal with their anger? What did they say or do?

How about the other kids? What kind of anger was acceptable among the boys, and among the girls, in the school setting? Were there different rules for boys and girls? Do you remember any single event about someone at school expressing anger? And what do you remember learning about the similarities or differences between how adults and children express anger?

Always keep yourself in focus no matter what scenarios you remember. What was your reaction to the situation? What did you usually say or do when people were showing their anger either directly to you or to someone else? You probably developed some reflex reactions, like wanting to leave the scene, wanting to cry, holding back tears, tensing up, or wanting to help so people would quit being angry.

Isn't it interesting to think back at the many ways in which the important adults in our lives taught us, even when they weren't trying? Isn't it amazing how many lessons are learned, without anyone being aware of something being taught and learned?

The same is true of partners or spouses. They have learned their own sets of lessons based on their experiences, and their reactions, like yours, were developed early on.

It is useful to spend some time thinking about these early lessons. Remember, anything that was learned can be un-learned. New responses can be learned, but first there must be an awareness of what is currently happening and why.

You might want to add to the list you started above regarding lessons learned at home and school about anger. Whether you make a list or not, try talking this topic over with either your spouse or a friend. They may become interested in the topic and join in with their own memories. They may not. Sharing your memories and insights will be good for you and might inadvertently encourage the listeners to do some retrospective thinking of their own.

Try to Understand Your Partner's Experience of Anger

Adults abused as children frequently feel different, defective, or strange. Growing up, they were often alone with their thoughts and feelings. Being little, they could not understand or explain the abuse; most abused children end up believing they are abused because they are bad, because they deserve the abuse, or because there is something inherently wrong with them. These belief systems can be very strong and can last for a very long time.

You may only see the person you love. You may know his or her strengths, and beauty. It may be hard for you to understand that even though you love and treat your partner with respect, he or she continues to be afraid or hesitant. You must try to put yourself in your partner's shoes.

Tell your partner that you've been thinking about your own childhood and the lessons you learned about the expression of anger. Then say that you would like to understand better what his or her childhood experience with anger was like. Since your request is made by first expressing your thoughts about yourself and your childhood, your partner may feel able to respond. You might also suggest that if it is difficult to communicate verbally, you will read anything your partner writes down.

Take whatever information your partner gives you and spend some time thinking about what it might have been like to grow up with these different experiences. If you have limited information, or no information at all, think about the types of abuse that have already been discussed and imagine what children of different ages would say or do given those circumstances. Put yourself in their shoes, trying to feel their feelings, and think their thoughts. You may or may not be one hundred percent accurate, but frequently these efforts result in increased insight.

One husband of a survivor told me, "Once I visualized the size difference between a child of six and her father, and once I actually could imagine how loud an adult's voice could be to a child, it was much easier for me to understand why she would run away as soon as I raised my voice slightly."

He went on to say that understanding this helped him feel less resentful toward his wife. "I used to get furious at her for confusing me with him. . . . I would never hit her or hurt her, and I resented her thinking I could."

Tell Each Other What Each of You Would Like Regarding Anger

Adult survivors usually grow up in families where communication is limited or nonexistent. It's as if each family member is isolated from the other, and no emotional contact is made. This environment does not encourage people to acknowledge their feelings or express their needs. Children learn to keep their needs or wants safely tucked away. Asking for things is a risky proposition. Some children pretend to want nothing,

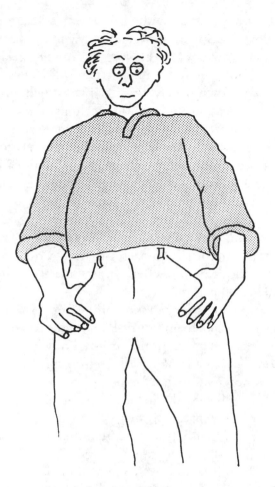

Once I visualized the size difference between a child of six and her father . . .

and avoid feelings of disappointment. This pretending helps them survive, but results in a great deal of longing.

Adult survivors need to identify what their needs are, and then how to ask to have those needs met. Talking these things over in a nonthreatening and serene way and describing desired behaviors may help each person get his or her needs met.

One of the needs of individuals in intimate relationships is to know how to resolve conflict and how to express anger in safe and appropriate ways. Having an intimate relationship means that both you and your partner will have a range of feelings toward each other, almost always including anger. To imagine a relationship without feelings of anger is very unrealistic. Anger will surface in all intimate relationships. Unfortunately, some people believe that if a relationship is healthy or happy, people won't get angry with each other. The opposite is true. A healthy and happy relationship allows for the safe and direct expression of anger.

Make sure that all discussions are begun during calm states when both you and your partner or spouse are able and willing to talk and listen to each other. **Do not enter into discussions about anger when angry at each other or in the middle of an argument.**

Before any discussions, take some time to think about what you would like from yourself and your partner regarding anger. Imagine a situation that you know tends to make you feel angry. Now imagine yourself in this situation, and think about how you **usually** express your anger. If you are completely satisfied with the way you handle your anger, and the way you express it, then you're ahead of the game. However, if you are not fully satisfied, then think about how you would like to handle your feelings of anger. Don't distract yourself with reasons why you can't behave in a desired way. For example, I was talking to the husband of a survivor once and asked him to do this exercise. He said, "Well what I would like to do is just tell her that I'm pissed off, raise my voice a little, and then let it be over; the problem is that anytime I say anything to her about how I feel, she immediately assumes I'm going to leave her, and she starts crying." This is not the time to distract yourself with how your partner or spouse might react. Think only about how you want to behave. Practice doing it a couple of times in your mind. Mentally rehearsing the desired behavior can be very valuable.

Now that you've spent some time thinking about what you'd like from yourself, think about a situation you know makes your partner angry. Think about what he or she **usually** does. What's your reaction to this? Can you listen and respond? Or would another approach make it easier for you to respond? If so, think about how you would like your partner to show you his or her anger. As you imagine your partner doing this, what's your response? How do things turn out?

If you and your partner have been talking about anger, and if you have shared your insights about yourself and your childhood lessons, you may now want to share how you would like to handle your angry feelings with your spouse. Tell him or her the situation you imagined and how you would like to behave.

If your partner is receptive, you may want to reveal how you hope he or she may be able to express anger at you. If you have decided to talk about this part, be sure that you approach the discussion in a nonaccusatory way as described in Chapter 6, on communication.

One couple I worked with had a real dilemma. He came from a large family in which he was the eldest of nine children. As such, his job was to take care of the younger kids. He was prone to yelling so that he could be heard over the loud rumblings of his brothers and sisters. His wife had grown up with both a father and grandfather who were drunk as well as physically and sexually abusive. Her way of living in that unsafe and chaotic family was to become extremely compliant and quiet. When they met each other, she was attracted by his caretaking, gentle ways, and he was attracted by her quiet compliance.

They had a good marriage. Once their children were born, the troubles began. Their parenting styles clashed, particularly regarding discipline. Predictably, he was boisterous and somewhat aggressive with the children; she was overprotective of the children, constantly pleading with him to "pipe down." Her constant pleadings infuriated him because he saw himself as loud but certainly not abusive! He felt she was undermining his relationship with the children, and she felt he was frightening the children. (In fact the children did not appear frightened by their father, but the mother did.)

In doing this exercise, the husband was able first to envision, and then describe to his wife, what he wanted from her. At the same time she was able to imagine and then tell him what she hoped for. Amazingly enough, their goals were very similar. He wanted to be able to discuss with her what to do when the kids did something wrong. He wanted them to arrive at a mutual decision and then back each other up. He said that when he was growing up he had had too much responsibility for his brothers and sisters, and had always wanted some help from his mother. She was shocked by the fact that he wanted to make joint decisions; she had thought of him as a dictator, for whom negotiation did not exist. She very much wanted to be able to talk over any problems with the children, but she felt that he would not respond. She was able to tell him how frightened she became when he yelled at the children, and acknowledged she was having a reflex response. She told him that it would be easier for her to talk with him if he kept his voice down. He agreed to try to keep his voice down, and she agreed to try to stop jumping to the defense of the children, since she began to see him as a safe and appropriate parent. Visualizing possible solutions to their problem was the first step. The second step for this couple was to put these solutions into practice and develop them into habits.

Practice When You're Not Angry

I can't emphasize enough how scary it can be for adult survivors to encounter angry feelings, words, and behaviors, particularly from people they love and trust. Even when they intellectually understand that they are "reacting," and want to behave differently, they are locked into behavior patterns by their childhood memories. Changes for adult survivors may come very slowly, because memories of childhood experiences and associated feelings well up so quickly and with power. Because of this, if the two of you are attempting to practice new ways of dealing with anger, try to practice during calm states. This kind of practicing is an opportunity to build new habits and mold the new behaviors you have imagined and mentally rehearsed. After each practice, evaluate how you did. Be sure you give yourself credit for what you accomplished.

Your spouse may or may not be available to practice with you. Do what you can for yourself. The goal is not to change your partner, but to encourage you to look at what you can do to change or improve the way you express your anger within the partnership.

In the above example, practicing was not easy. The husband continued to have an instinct to yell for a long time; the wife had the urge to protect her children more often than she expected. They practiced both during an upset and at other times. Sometimes when they were both calm and happy, he would practice speaking in a low, nonthreatening voice, and she would practice telling him the ways in which he and her father were different people, even though they both had a loud voice.

Define High-Risk Situations and Trigger Words

To make the relationship feel more safe for the adult survivor, it is important to explore what creates an unsafe environment. For example, screaming or a spouse's walking out during an argument may elicit great fear. Some behaviors that can provoke fear in adult survivors may be unknown or undefined until they occur. However, a careful exploration may pinpoint some of the trigger areas.

If you and your spouse or partner have been expressing anger in an aggressive way, the first thing to do is to try to cool things down. Pick a time when you are getting along well and talk together about how you are handling anger in the relationship.

First, define the situations or words that have triggered trouble in the past. Make an agreement that you will not rehash old arguments now, but simply understand what kinds of things have caused problems in the past. You will be charting a course for how to express anger safely by avoiding the situations, behaviors, or words that can cause an argument to turn to a full-blown (unsafe) fight.

Because angry behavior and angry words have occurred without resolution, they remain sensitive to new eruptions. Don't try to resolve past problems immediately. You first try to develop some new ways of dealing with anger, then you try to tackle the "old issues" with a new approach.

One way to cool things down is to work on avoiding angry outbursts. To avoid them, it is useful to define situations or words that trigger angry explosions. Here's a list one couple made out about situations, behaviors, or words that usually led to explosive outbursts of anger:

His
When I'm tired
When I get home from work

When I'm drinking
When I've got a deadline at work
When I haven't spent time with the guys

Hers
When I'm tired
When we haven't gone out together for more than a
    month
When he's drinking
When he doesn't talk to me

Here's their list of trigger words (or phrases):

His
Why don't you talk to me?
What's wrong with you?
When can we get away?
Jerkwad

Hers
What's for dinner?
Didn't you go shopping yet?
You're soooo tired

It doesn't really matter (initially) why these situations or words carry the impact they do. The important thing is to work on avoiding them.

Some negotiations might take place. The wife who made the list above may decide to accept the fact that when her husband is working on a deadline they will not be going out. At the same time, she may want to schedule something shortly after the deadline is met. That way she has something to look forward to and doesn't need to feel resentful. The husband, understanding that his wife feels neglected when he's working on a deadline, might decide to schedule a special date or trip for himself and his wife at a time when he expects to complete the project. This kind of negotiation helps both parties.

If certain words or phrases are particularly upsetting to one or the other, attempts can be made to strike the words from the vocabulary. This is hard to do, and it may take a number of slips before the word or phrase disappears completely. People make mistakes and learn from them. Changes occur only when efforts are made.

This kind of negotiating works when both spouses are clear that they do not want to continue expressing anger in the same old problematic way. Both people agree they are not happy with the way they show anger, even though they may not like it for totally different reasons.

Talk About Out-of-Control Anger

One of the most terrifying situations to survivors of abuse is anger expressed in an out-of-control way. It is absolutely critical to make sure that this type of problem is controlled rapidly and efficiently.

Out-of-control anger happens when people feel their anger gets the best of them; they feel they cannot control their words or behavior. They say things like "I don't know what got into me" or "Before I knew it I was screaming terrible things in a very loud voice." They describe outbursts that seem to surface without provocation, yet interestingly enough, out-of-control anger expression has usually been brewing for some time and feelings of helplessness and despair have loomed large.

Out-of-control anger can be described as "blowing off steam," and a useful analogy is that of a kettle boiling and "popping its lid." This kind of anger explosion usually comes after a great deal of frustration and buildup. Usually, the individual has been "storing up" small resentments and frustrations, without taking the time to feel or vent the angry feelings in appropriate ways. The individual can suddenly become explosive over a minor problem, seemingly overreacting.

One spouse told me that she didn't really understand how she could become so rageful. She used words such as *suddenly, without notice, before I knew it.* One night she had experienced an angry outburst and had thrown a vase at her husband. (He had grown up with an abusive parent, and these situations made him feel desperate and depressed.)

When this woman and I explored her outburst, it became clear to both of us that there was nothing sudden about her anger. She described a full two weeks of being frustrated almost daily, feeling that her spouse was avoiding her since he was coming home late and traveling more than usual. She was beginning to suspect he was having an affair. (In fact, her husband was staying away more than usual to avoid getting into more fights, not because he was having an affair.) In addition to her problems with her husband, this woman had work and health pressures. Her disappointments and stress had become cumulative and the buildup had resulted in an outburst. Once she delineated her own pattern of frustration buildup and resulting explosiveness, she was able to define some ways to diffuse problems, which included a daily "checking-in" with her husband as well as a daily record-keeping of both positive and negative feelings, to be shared at an agreed-upon time.

If you have experienced out-of-control anger, it's important to try to look at how to "catch yourself," during the buildup phase and before the explosion.

It helps first to:

• Notice the physical signs of anger, such as headaches, stomachaches, painful shoulders or neck, etc.

- Notice phrases you say to yourself when you start feeling angry, like *don't let it get to you,* or *just let it go,* or *easy does it.*
- Notice your feelings. Do you feel frustrated, irritable, depressed?
- Notice your general outlook. Do you want to get up in the morning, do you look forward to work, to coming home? Do you notice you're dragging?
- Notice your interactions with friends and family. Do you find yourself getting annoyed at people you care about, do you jump down their throats at the slightest provocation?
- Notice your perceptions. Are you feeling accused, attacked, defensive? Do you think others are out to get you? If you're feeling any or all of the above, it is a clue to slow down and spend some time figuring out what's bothering you. Identify what's causing the irritability. Don't push down or push away your angry feelings. You're not doing anyone a favor by avoiding the problem. It's better for you and others if you look your angry feelings square in the face. Then take some action to express the anger safely and relieve some of the pressure. It is much easier to stop the pressure before it has the chance to gain momentum.

If the out-of-control anger is a major way through which you and your spouse communicate, it is best to seek outside help. These are powerful patterns that are difficult to change.

Create Nonverbal Signals and Alternatives

If fights have become commonplace in your relationship, it might also help to develop some nonverbal ways of diffusing an argument or nipping it in the bud. It is not always possible to talk when you feel angry. The best of intentions can go out the window when anger enters the picture. So until you are expert enough at dealing with your anger as well as you would like, you can give each other signals without talking. For example, you may just signal "time out" with some manual gesture like making a *T* with your hands.

This signal means that you are getting angry, you need a time out, and you will return when you've cooled down. This will only work if you and your partner have discussed this and you both understand that you are not "walking out" or "abandoning ship," and that you are willing to discuss the problem further as soon as you feel more composed.

One couple had a creative way of nonverbal communication. They cut out little red and green square cards. When they felt angry and could not talk to each other, they pulled out a card. The red card meant, "Stop. Something is hurting me right now and I can't talk. I'll talk to you as soon as I can. I need time out." The green card meant, "This is going to be a difficult conversation, but I am willing to try to communi-

You may just signal "Time Out."

cate with you now." Each signal expressed a particular need, whether it was to take some time out, or to proceed with caution because the topic was sensitive. Whatever the signal, the intent is the same: to slow things down. Slowing things down means eventually problems are addressed.

The problems must be discussed as soon as possible, and not forgotten. It is helpful if one or the other partner writes down the topic and keeps a list of things to discuss at an appropriate time. Many couples set aside time for weekly meetings in which problematic issues are addressed.

Never Let Anger Build Up (Like Steam in a Kettle)

It is worth repeating that one of the worst things you can do is let anger go unexpressed.

Make sure that you don't let too much time go by without addressing your concern (no more than a day) and certainly try never to go to bed angry. At the very least give the message, "I am upset right now and I'm finding it hard to talk, but I promise as soon as I can, I'll try to talk with you about it some more." Another possibility is "I'm feeling angry right now, and anger is just another feeling. . . . I care about you and I know we'll be able to work this out." Anger can be frightening to a lot of people, and these reassurances can help the situation. If you find it hard to talk, pass your partner a note.

Use Your Body to Release Anger

When you are angry, your body knows it. You can feel tense, have aches and pains, breathe differently, and have a change in blood pressure.

Give your body a chance to release some energy in whatever way you like. Run, do jumping jacks, use a trampoline, play tennis, go for a brisk walk, or do any form of physical exercise that's convenient. This is a legitimate and healthy way of expressing anger, and it is best done in combination with other direct ways of expressing anger, that is, talking it over with your partner or a friend.

To illustrate this point, you might want to take a brisk walk and while you do, ask yourself, "What am I feeling hurt or angry about?" and "What can I do to make myself feel better?" Once you figure out what you're angry about, you might want to make statements to yourself or out loud while you walk. "I deserve to be angry. That person was not respectful. I am angry because that person didn't ask me what I did, she just assumed I made the mistake." Say it a few times and mean it. You are entitled to feel angry. You don't have to justify the feeling of anger. Acknowledge the presence of anger and decide the best way to release it.

When you ask yourself the question about what would make you feel better, generate a few options. Having choices will always make you feel more powerful. Think through what will happen if you make any of the choices at hand. Then make a decision and follow through.

Following through might mean role-playing what you want to say, writing a letter you send or don't send, making a phone call, or confronting the person directly. Direct confrontations do not have to be abusive or angry. It helps to say how you feel, and ask for something specific. As I mention in Chapter 6, on communication, "I" statements make it easier for the person to listen.

Express Anger in Safe Ways

Adult survivors don't know, and frequently can't imagine, how to express anger safely. The abusive ways of expressing anger are familiar. They may be surprised to hear there are other ways of expressing anger, and may express disbelief at the idea that anger is just another emotion, which can be expressed in nonhurtful ways. I have found it useful to make some definitive statements to adult survivors even though these statements may not be immediately credible. I like to tell survivors that it is not okay to hit or hurt children, and that children do not have to be hit to be disciplined. Because these are foreign concepts, it helps to repeat these ideas frequently.

You may want to say, "It is not okay to hit or hurt people with fists or words as a way of showing anger." I also encourage you to make some general statements about acceptable ways of showing anger, such as talking directly to the person in a nonaccusatory way. Give your spouse an example of how you will talk to him or her when you are angry. "When you do or say [whatever] I feel angry. What makes me angry is [whatever]. I wish instead of doing or saying [whatever] you would try doing this instead"; or, "we need to figure out how we're going to deal with this in a different way." The final and important thing to remember about anger is that feeling angry is okay; how it is expressed is what makes it good or bad.

If you are not able to talk about anger directly with your partner, you can talk to a friend. If friends are not available, you might want to try writing down your thoughts and feelings. Perhaps sometime you will want to share your writings with your partner.

To summarize, anger can be expressed directly as stated above, or in less direct ways, such as "role-playing" what you want to say, and "acting out" the communication. You can also mentally rehearse what you want to say or do.

Physical exercise can also help relieve some of the tension your body feels when you are angry.

The primary goal is to express anger in a safe and direct way. To do so, you must acknowledge the anger, accept it as a normal feeling, prepare yourself to deal with anger, practice desired behaviors, develop alternatives to explosive or violent expressions of anger, know the clues of anger buildup, and deal with anger either directly or indirectly.

Summary

Adult survivors of childhood abuse did not learn normal and safe ways of expressing anger. For them, the emotion of anger may be life-threatening, and intellectual understanding of their responses may not help them feel more comfortable with angry feelings.

Anger is almost always a normal part of intimate relationships. As a matter of fact, the more trust and love exists, the safer it will be for anger to be expressed.

Living with, or loving, people who are deathly afraid of anger requires sensitive and careful attention. Adult survivors must become familiar with the emotion of anger and its expression. They may be doing some of this work in their own therapy.

As a partner or a spouse, you can help by (1) taking some time to understand your own thoughts and actions regarding anger expression, (2) taking time to understand your partner's current fears and hesitations, (3) behaving in appropriate and safe ways.

This chapter has discussed ways in which you can begin to explore your thoughts and feelings about anger, envision and practice desired behaviors, and share with your partner what you have learned. This sharing may in turn help create a safe environment for your partner to explore his or her feelings about anger and how it is expressed.

Chapter 2

TOUCHING

The Fear/Wish of Touching and Being Touched

Sometimes I go to my room and in the dark, I stroke my hair. I just ache for him to touch me gently, lovingly. I just wish he could be relaxed about hugging and being physically close. I can see his body tense up when I come near him and it breaks my heart.

Touching is as necessary to survival as food. All humans require and thrive on physical nurturing. Depending on childhood experiences, the willingness to initiate touch, the expectation and desire for it, and the comfort with touch will differ.

Survivors of abuse have a particularly difficult time with touch; they have experienced unsafe, unwanted, and intrusive touch. Survivors of physical abuse and neglect experienced the extremes of touch: violence and deprivation. Survivors of sexual abuse have limited experiences with nonsexual touching; they may be unaware of nurturing, affectionate, or playful touch.

When young children are abused, they are unable to protect themselves fully; they cannot run away, hide, seek shelter, or fight back. They rely on psychological self-protection. Abused children develop and use psychological ways of protecting against harm or pain, and while the defenses work initially, they can interfere with adult functioning. The defenses become reflex responses that do not always discriminate between real and perceived threats.

We learn a great deal about instinctive protection from observing animals in the wild. When threatened, they employ one of three basic buffers: They flee, fight, or "play possum." Taking flight or fighting are visible defenses; playing possum requires the animal to blend into the environment, go limp, or appear defeated in order to escape. Abused children use similar defenses; since their abilities to flee or fight successfully are restricted, the most common defense is to "play possum" by pretending to sleep, going limp, going numb, or being physically unresponsive. Therapists call this ability to escape emotionally **dissociation.** Dissociation is described by people who do it as "spacing out," "going inside," or "getting little." There are many ways people dissociate.

I once worked with a ten-year-old physically abused child who had been abused since the age of two. I was going to drive her somewhere and she got into the car first and then I went to the driver's seat and noticed that she was bent down in the passenger's seat. I asked her why she was bent over and she calmly stated, "My fingers are in the door." I immediately opened the door and tried to comfort her. Her eyes were fixed as she said, "Big girls don't cry." I took her to the emergency room and she showed absolutely no signs of discomfort as she was examined and treated. This was the first time I had seen anyone with the incredible ability to detach totally from pain. And yet, given her history, it was to be expected. She had learned to numb herself whenever she felt pain; she could disconnect from it effectively. At the

Therapists call this ability to escape emotionally "dissociation."

same time that this technique was effective, it also caused her some problems. For example, in this instance it would have been possible for me to drive to my destination without knowing that she was in distress. She could have lost her fingers due to her ability to detach from the pain and from reality; she was unable to ask for help because she was unable to feel the pain. While this detaching technique had helped this child get through painful beatings at home, it had serious drawbacks, particularly when the defense surfaced in response to a variety of situations, not just threatening ones. One survivor of sexual abuse told me that she was currently in a loving, safe relationship and yet when her lover reached over to touch her, she could not stay in her body. Therefore, she could not make the intimate contact she now wanted because psychologically she defended herself against **the possibility** of being hurt when anyone touched her.

People use many different kinds of emotional responses to protect themselves against unwanted or unsafe touch, but two of the most common are the kind of numbing described above, and hyperalertness.

Hyperalertness is also used to feel safe and protected. The individual who uses this type of psychological defense is always on the alert, always scanning the environment, always ready to react. An individual who is hyperalert and hypervigilant uses up a great deal of physical and psychic energy because the body is always prepared to fight, flee, or numb out. Consequently, there is physical tension and tightening of the muscles. The body and mind become fatigued from constant anticipation of attack. If someone is constantly hypervigilant, it is difficult for them to stay available for human contact and stay emotionally present. While this defense can feel helpful to the individual, a high emotional price is paid.

People with abusive backgrounds enter adulthood with specific worries, fears, and expectations. They have learned reflexes that will continue to exist unless they are identified, understood, dislodged, and replaced. This is not an impossible task, but it can be difficult and it takes a great deal of practice.

As a partner, spouse, or friend of an adult survivor, there are several ways in which you can understand and regard the problem of touching. Here are several suggestions:

- It's not a matter of right and wrong
- Depersonalize
- Understand the underlying difficulty
- Broaden the types of touching used
- Differentiate between nurturing and sexual touch
- Learn how to communicate about touching in general
- Learn how to ask for what you want specifically
- Practice asking and giving
- Have "touching sessions" to increase the level of comfort

• Remember, touching habits take time to form and become second-nature

It's Not a Matter of Right and Wrong

Always remember that if your partner has difficulty with touching, it doesn't mean she or he is wrong and you are right. All it means is that you have had different experiences with touching in the past that now shape your willingness, desire, and comfort with touch. It is very important that your partner is not made to feel defective or inadequate due to discomfort or fear of touch. It will help a lot if you can approach the subject gently, talk about what you would like to see happen, and affirm your willingness to help and be patient. You can write a letter, make a tape recording, or talk directly to your partner. What you say may go something like this:

> I'm really glad that we're together. I think we make a good couple, and I'm happy that we met and came to have a relationship. The more I know you, the more I love you. And the more time we spend together, the more I learn about you and me together as a couple. One thing I have noticed is that sometimes when I reach out to touch you, you seem to be uncomfortable. Sometimes you get very still; other times you push my hand away gently. I would like us to talk together about touching, so I can understand how you feel about it, and so we can figure out how to touch so it feels good and loving and safe to both of us.

You notice that in this suggested message I start out with a positive comment about the relationship. When your partner hears this, she or he will probably feel more receptive to what follows. Next, I state clearly what has been noticed in behavioral terms. There is a difference between saying "Sometimes when I reach out you get very still; other times you push my hand away gently" and "Sometimes when I reach out you get cold and distant and you don't want me to touch you anymore." In the first statement the behavior is described, in the second statement an **interpretation** of the observed behavior is given. This can make your partner feel accused or judged in some way. You also run the risk of making a mistake; pushing your hand away gently does not necessarily mean that your partner does not want you (specifically) to touch him or her.

The next important message I emphasize above is that I am willing to work on understanding what the problem is, and on resolving the problem together. This way your partner does not feel singled out as the one with the problem, and the one who has to make the change. You convey a desire to work with your partner toward a goal that will be mutually beneficial.

Survivors are very sensitive to being wrong or bad. They may harbor feelings of worthlessness and be very sensitive to hearing others' disappointments. Survivors can also be quick to assume that they are not good enough and feel deeply hurt by their inadequacies. Keeping this in mind while preparing your approach is very helpful. At the same time, you are absolutely right to want to talk about any problem between you and your spouse or partner, and to want to improve and enhance your ongoing relationship.

Depersonalize

Probably the hardest thing for partners, spouses, and friends to do is to depersonalize the survivor's behavior. Often, partners feel frustrated, angry, or confused when they think that the survivor is responding to them personally rather than to the situation.

Mark and Marge were married for six years. Mark was a

survivor of physical and emotional abuse and he had struggled for many years to decrease his negative impulses. During his younger years he had a drinking problem and got into bar brawls with regularity. He had been fired from his first four jobs because, as he described it, he "couldn't control his temper." As he got older, things calmed down. He was always in control of his emotions, and as a matter of fact, he had become somewhat overcontrolled, something his wife complained about. She would often state that living with Mark was like living with a "man of stone," who never seemed to have strong feelings about anything. She was most concerned that she often felt disregarded or ignored by him, and there were times she felt that she was unattractive to him.

Marge had tried and tried to get Mark to be more expressive and show enthusiasm in different situations. Out of frustration, she had resorted to loud outbursts of anger. She sometimes yelled harsh words to him, and hearing these words reminded Mark of verbal abuse from his own parents. When this occurred, Mark retreated further and felt resentful and angry toward Marge. Since anger was no longer a permissible emotion for Mark, he simply withdrew further and further. He became more depressed and unresponsive, and Marge responded with increased abuse. The marriage was in serious danger. Marge and Mark retreated into their own physical and emotional space and the distance between them grew larger.

Both Mark and Marge had to learn to depersonalize what was going on. Marge needed to develop a new perspective on Mark's withdrawal; he was not uninterested in her, he was trying to keep himself controlled and safe from violent outbursts. Marge was not verbally attacking Mark because she did not love him; she was attempting to spark a response in him. The first step, therefore, was to depersonalize the problematic behavior and give it a new meaning that was less personal, and more a response to the situation.

Marge and Mark loved each other very much. However, by the time they were in crisis, both of them were burned out and feeling hopeless. Once they were able to affirm their mutual love, and made a commitment to work on their mutual problem, they were on their way to doing two important things: breaking down the familiar, unhealthy patterns and creating some new, positive, and healthy patterns.

Of course, it's always better to catch the problems early on before the distance grows and the helplessness begins. One of the best ways to do that is to pay attention to your feelings, discuss any problems that surface early on, and learn to depersonalize your partner's behavior, always assuming that there is probably an underlying situational trigger.

Understand the Underlying Difficulty

Trying to figure out what's causing the problem is easier said than done. It's important for you to remember that you are not **causing** the problem, and yet you may be able to do or say something that alleviates or diffuses it.

You can make guesses at what the underlying problem is, or you can offer suggestions, but your partner will have to be the one to confirm your guesses or suggestions, or to tell you more about the nature of the problem. A few things are worth noting here: Your partner will have to feel safe and comfortable enough to talk to you, and you can't pressure someone into feeling safe and comfortable. Also, your partner may not know or understand what's causing the problematic feeling and response. Your partner and you may need to spend some time considering possibilities, or you may need to get an objective view from someone you trust.

Even if the underlying problem is not fully discovered or understood, attempts toward reducing or bypassing the problem can be productive.

Broaden the Types of Touching Used

There are many types of touching. In close relationships people can hug, embrace, hold each other, or caress in order to communicate inner feelings. Touching is not always serious in nature; there are touches that are playful and fun. Sometimes touching is purposeful, such as when touch is a way to initiate sexual contact, or when it is used to alleviate pain, for example, when one person gives another a soothing massage.

Since survivors are more than likely unfamiliar with the range of touching, it is important for them to have the opportunity to learn about these possibilities.

One way to convey this information is to discuss it together. I'll talk about this a little later in this chapter. Another way to convey information about touching is by actually demonstrating types of touching in a gentle, nonthreatening way. Select an activity that might include some nonintrusive touching and ask your spouse to participate. For example, as silly as it might sound, you may buy some finger paints and some paper and have some fun. Show what you accomplished to your partner. He or she may want to try a painting; if your partner doesn't volunteer, you may ask him or her to join in with you. If you do a finger painting together, you will be touching in a playful and nonthreatening manner. If your partner responds well, you might put your hands together and make a joint finger painting.

Another touching exercise that can be fun is to face each other, hold your hands out, and place your hands together with all fingertips touching. Decide who will lead and who will follow. The person who leads then moves his or her hands around while the other person follows. The lead is exchanged.

As you can see, I am focusing on touching that is not

. . . another touching exercise

intrusive, agitated, or threatening. The types of touching can become more intimate as time goes on. Types of touching that are extreme, such as wrestling or pushing, or tickling, are not recommended. Be careful to avoid holding down, pushing down, or exerting any force. This is good advice with anyone; with survivors it is critical.

Differentiate Between Nurturing and Sexual Touch

Survivors of sexual abuse or incest need special care. They have experienced sexuality in an abusive, intrusive, and unpleasant way. They are usually confused at best, and can harbor feelings of fear and trepidation about any type of touching. These feelings will be discussed in more detail in the next chapter on sexuality, but for now, it is sufficient to say that sexual touching needs to be differentiated from nurturing touch. Make sure that you and your partner have considered the differences, because often survivors avoid all types of touch, perceiving it as a precursor to sex or violence.

Again, the discussion must occur in a calm and cautious way. You need to bring it up as something that is of interest to you. Your approach may go something like this:

> I wanted to let you know how much I love it when we are close to each other and when we touch. I was thinking to myself the other day that there are so many ways to touch, not just touching when we want to make love. Sometimes I just want to touch you or hold you, and I don't necessarily want to make love. I'd like to be able to tell you when I want to touch or snuggle without making love. Maybe we can figure out a way we can signal each other. Maybe sometimes you just want to cuddle or be close and you don't want to make love. I'd love just to cuddle and be close with you. Maybe we can figure out a way to let each other know.

As you can see in this example, I start out by being positive about the relationship. A less useful way to begin a discussion like this would be "We're not touching enough for my taste. I want you to feel more comfortable when I come near you." The difference is that in my example, there is an assertion of love first, and an affirmation of the things that are enjoyed. I then proceed to talk **about myself**, not about my partner. I talk about what **I** was thinking about, what **I** would like to have happen. I then bring up that my partner may actually want some similar things. Lastly, the solution will be **mutually** discussed. My partner will not be told what to do or say.

Learn How to Communicate About Touching in General

Sometimes, talking about touching can feel scary to survivors and nonsurvivors. People in relationships can feel vulnerable to feelings of rejection and inadequacy. Survivors in particular can feel sensitive to having done something wrong.

Communicating to your partner about touching in general must be done with care.

I think a good way to begin the dialogue is by approaching your friend or partner stating that you have recently been thinking about touching and your feelings about touching and being touched. Share with your partner some of what you learned about touching as a child. You might ask your partner if it's okay for you to talk about touching a little. If your partner is willing to listen, you might start by talking about your parents, caretakers, or siblings, and touching you noticed in your family. Share times in your life when you liked or didn't like touching, or what you've learned about your preferences. Talk about your own level of comfort with touch. This is a natural lead-in to reviewing out loud what kinds of physical contact you are familiar with. Notice if your partner is comfortable or attentive as you speak. If he or she shows signs of discomfort or uninterest, cut your discussion short and make it clear you will try again some other time. It's almost always best to talk about yourself. This will encourage your partner to volunteer information. Avoid being inquisitive or challenging. Also, keep from making accusations or generalizations. A rule of thumb is to avoid using words such as "always" or "never." Make sure you sprinkle lots of positives throughout the conversation, making clear statements about what you like about your partner, how positive or happy you have felt in your relationship, and how you look forward to a future together. Always remember to notice how your partner reacts to what you're saying. Give him or her an opportunity to speak, and always end the communication by doing two things: Thank your partner for listening, and express your willingness to listen in return.

Learn How to Ask for What You Want Specifically

Survivors of sexual abuse are individuals who struggle with feelings of low self-esteem; vulnerable to feelings of self-doubt and self-recrimination, they are likely to perceive rejections or accusations easily. Because of this, it is important for your communication to be as clear as possible. This will prevent unnecessary pain and confusion.

If you want to approach your partner to ask for more cuddling, do so in a plain fashion, bypassing the use of broad generalizations. Avoid statements that express disappointment or anger. For example, starting with a statement like "Things just aren't working out" might get unwanted results. Your partner may become defensive (as a result of feeling attacked), or worse, may withdraw and be unavailable for further discussion, leaving you feeling frustrated. It's best to think through how to phrase your communication so it is both positive (as demonstrated earlier) and **specific** to your needs. A better approach would be: "Honey, I love it when we cuddle. I feel so warm and close to you. I would love it if we cuddled more frequently. What do you think?" This way, there is little doubt that you are asking to increase the frequency of cuddling. You might want to practice this way of communicating when you make requests. "I love your tuna casserole. I'd love to eat it more frequently if you're willing to make it" is certainly clearer than "You never make things that I like to eat." Like anything else, the more you communicate in this way, the easier it will seem, and the more you will be able to judge the impact of good communication.

Practice Asking and Giving

Survivors of childhood abuse probably received sparse or inconsistent physical or emotional affection. Abusive parents may have felt uncomfortable touching their children, or they may have turned to them to get their own needs met. Abusive parents may have demanded physical affection from their children when they were upset or angry or frightened, and the children may have complied out of fear or obligation. In addition, survivors may have met parental demands expecting attention or affection in return. When children have these early confusing associations with giving and receiving, they do not develop comfort with these exchanges, and they are certainly not given the opportunity to choose freely. Caring for another because it is a way to avoid being beaten is drastically different than caring for another because it feels good to give and receive affection.

Survivors need to develop a tolerance for accepting positive attention or affection from their partners. As a friend or partner, you will need to be steady in your gentleness **and** perseverance. At first you may need to give and then ask your partner what is was like to receive something unexpectedly. When you give your partner something, like flowers, it might be a good idea to put your gift into words. For example, if you bring him or her flowers you might say, "Today I was thinking of you and how happy I feel that we're together. I thought about how kind you are and how much I love the way we laugh together. I wanted to bring you a little something that would show you I was thinking about you." When you do this, you are offering a gift of love and affection and clearly stating the message that the gift represents.

When you receive something, whether it's tangible such as a gift, or more elusive such as a warm feeling of being loved, let your partner know what it's like for you to have this experience. What I am encouraging here is that the topic of giving and receiving be discussed openly, so that survivors are encouraged to consider their thoughts and feelings about these interactions. In the process of your open discussion, you are also accomplishing something more: You are developing some guidelines for asking and responding to requests, and these guidelines will serve you well as your relationship flourishes. Remember that good habits are as easy to build as bad ones.

Have "Touching Sessions" to Increase Level of Comfort

I am putting this suggestion toward the end of this chapter because I encourage you to hold back from unfamiliar physical experimenting until both of you are comfortable with nonthreatening and/or playful touch. At this juncture, you might want to talk with your partner about the possibility of "practicing" some hugging, cuddling, holding, and other forms of nonsexual touching. These types of touching elicit warm and intimate feelings between partners, and yet survivors will need to **build a tolerance** for positive behaviors.

On occasion, partners of survivors have had a negative response to this. David, who was married to Lara, a survivor of sexual and physical abuse, felt very hurt by the insinuation that Lara had to develop a tolerance to him! He had misinterpreted what I had said. I said that his wife had to build a tolerance to positive affection, not to him. She was very much in love with him. But when he held her, caressed her, and whispered in her ear, she became frightened and numb. When she felt her husband's arms around her, she felt threatened, entrapped. These feelings were reminiscent of those she had when she was sexually attacked by her father. She could not tolerate the closeness; she was not familiar with holding that did not lead to abusive touch. She had to learn to become comfortable and safe with the feelings aroused by safe touch. Her individual therapy was helpful along those lines, but equally helpful was David's willingness to understand that his wife, Lara, had negative associations to touching, and needed the time and support to develop new and positive associations.

As Lara developed a comfort with David's touch, she was less likely to go numb, or pretend she was not inside her body. Lara had learned to dissociate when she was physically or sexually abused as a child; she was now choosing to stay in the present and feel her feelings as they occurred. David and Lara both wanted Lara to stay emotionally available and present during touching. David learned to talk to his wife as he held her to keep her in the present. "Lara," he would say, "this is David, and we choose to be together, and we love each other. You like my smile and my sense of humor. I like your beauty, both inside and outside. We have a good life together. We make decisions together. We've got plans to go on vacation. I love to touch your skin. It's soft and warm. Talk to me, Lara." Lara would say, "David, I'm in your arms and I choose to be here. I like when you touch my arm. It tickles a little and makes me feel warm inside. We do have a beautiful life together, and I look forward to our relationship getting stronger all the time."

Both David and Lara reported how difficult and awkward it felt to talk to each other while they held and caressed. At the same time, they were surprised at how much they had to say to each other, and how close they felt after these touching exercises. They also reported that asserting their choice was extremely important, and there were times when one or the other did not feel in the mood to do the touching exercise, or did not feel in the mood to talk while touching. Any and all variations on this exercise were acceptable as long as both individuals were consenting each step of the way.

Remember, Touching Habits Take Time to Form and Become Second-Nature

Individuals who grow up in healthy, functional, and non-abusive families learn different and positive lessons as children. To them easy, playful, and loving touches are second-nature. They are not frightened by displays of physical affection. They respond in kind when touched by friends and partners. They do not retreat as a result of being touched; they reciprocate effortlessly.

This is very encouraging for you to know. It is clear that if people are given safety, love, security, and appropriate physical and emotional affection, they learn to respond accordingly. Touching becomes a rewarding experience.

In your intimate relationship with your partner, you must always be safe, appropriate, honest, and loving. Eventually, the survivor will sense the love and safety, will grow accustomed to it, will want to give and receive loving care, and the physical and emotional relationship you share will deepen.

Chapter 3

SEXUALITY

You're Damned If You Do,
Damned If You Don't

*Sometimes we're in the middle of making love and I can
feel her slip away. Her eyes glaze over, her body goes limp,
and she's just not there. I'm on my own and I hate it. I love
her and I want to work it out, but it feels hopeless. I hate
her old man for what he did, and I hate that she can't keep
us separate.*

Children are born sexual beings. There is a consensus among
professionals who study sexuality that individuals are born
with the capacity to be sexual, and that no one has to be
taught how to respond sexually, since the body has instinc-
tual responses to sexual stimulation. Sexologists also indicate
that while the sexual response is not learned, associations that
are made between arousal and circumstances that cause
arousal are learned. If early sexual contact is pleasant and
nonviolent, later arousal will most likely occur under these
conditions; arousal generated during unsafe and violent circumstances becomes associated with these conditions. If
arousal is experienced in an unsafe or violent way, later

arousal will most likely become associated with these conditions. Therefore, it makes sense that if early arousal has been followed by pain of some kind, a survivor striving to remain safe will avoid sexual arousal. This is a very important concept and helps to explain why survivors of sexual assault may avoid sexual activity, engage in robotlike sexual activity, need to be physically hurt or humiliated during sex, or may be flooded during lovemaking with memories of abuse.

Another important concept is that men or women who are sexually abused and traumatized have had the normal development of sexuality disturbed by abusive and traumatic events. Children develop physically, emotionally, cognitively, spiritually, **and** sexually as they grow. Sexual development is gradual and progressive in nature. Children's interest in sexuality evolves over time, and appears to go from self-exploration, to mutual exploration, to more sophisticated sexual interest based on experiences and stimulation.

Children who are sexually abused learn about sexuality prematurely. They usually have a range of feelings including confusion, doubt, pleasure, and pain, and have a need to make sense of the event. The problem is that the young child does not have the cognitive ability to understand sexuality, or the circumstances under which the sexual abuse is occurring. Frequently, sexually abused children are told to keep the sexual abuse a secret, or are threatened with harm if they reveal what is going on. Other times, the children inherently sense that the abuse is something to be kept secret. They may want it to stop but don't know how to make that happen.

Sexual abuse is a complex subject for adults to comprehend. Children are at a real disadvantage in their ability to make sense of what's going on. Physical abuse is more clear-cut: it hurts. Sexual abuse may have parts that feel bad and parts that feel good. The child's body can become aroused to sexual stimulation, and even young children can be masturbated to orgasm. An orgasm is a pleasant and intense sensation that a child can like very much, and want to have happen again.

Sexually abused children may feel immediately guilty for liking the sexual abuse, or as adults they may harbor massive feelings of guilt for this enjoyment. And yet adult survivors need to understand that it is okay to like pleasant physical sensations in the body, while not liking the sexual contact when it is incestuous. Survivors may feel that they didn't protest enough or that they could have asked for the abuse to stop. This is not the case. Sexually abused children **cannot** give informed consent. Some children and adults get very confused about this. They may think that if they didn't fight, or cry, or say *"No"* in one way or another, that they were saying *"Yes."* Nothing could be further from the truth. Children are not in a position to consent when, cognitively, they have limited ability to understand the parameters and implications of sexual contact.

Men and women who sexually abuse children are obviously much more sophisticated than their victims. They may say things like "If you don't like this, tell me and I'll stop," and further convince children that they are participating freely in the sexual abuse. Children cannot give consent, and any participation that others perceive should be understood in the context of the child's need to survive, be safe, be loved and nurtured. For example, a child may cooperate with requests or demands for sexual stimulation because the consequences of failing to comply are threats of physical harm to them or their loved ones.

One incestuous father would give his six-year-old daughter a great deal of physical affection immediately after his orgasm. He would not touch her at any other time. This child was in a bind. She disliked the sexual abuse, and left her body while it was going on, but she very much liked, and looked forward to, the hugging, kissing, and physical affection that followed the sexual act.

As you can see, the sexual abuse of a child can't help but affect the child's sexuality as an adult. All survivors of sexual abuse need to understand the experience and its impact on their adult sexuality. Survivors also face a range of feelings about sexuality long after the childhood abuse takes place. These feelings can cause the survivor a variety of unusual or extreme responses to sex, including physical numbing, self-injury to the body or genitals, sexual "dysfunctions," avoiding sex, yearning for sexual contact, seeking bizarre or violent sexual contact, seeking sex with unavailable partners, paying or getting paid for sex, arousal to pain or humiliation, and dangerous sex. Survivors are **not doomed** to these forms of sexuality. There is great hope for recovery from sexual problems such as those described above. Survivors can be helped to reclaim their sexuality, create new and positive associations to sex, and choose loving and positive sexual contact with lovers and spouses. Some of the work must be done by the survivor of sexual abuse. The following suggestions can be extremely helpful to you, as a sexual partner:

- Talk about your sexual history
- Talk about your understanding of sexual abuse
- Emphasize the importance of **making choices** about sex
- Assert the need for safe, loving sexual contact
- Express your interest in helping make sex safe and fun
- Talk about initiating sex
- Talk about how to stop sex once started
- Talk about likes and dislikes
- Talk about triggers
- Talk about dissociation

Talk About Your Sexual History

The subject of sexuality can be a threatening one for survivors of childhood sexual abuse who have probably associated sex with secrecy and shame for many years. The subject has to be introduced gently, without any expectations. Initially, you can approach your partner by sharing about yourself and your experiences. Here's an example of how you can go about this:

> Susan, I'd like to spend some time together talking. I've been thinking about my growing up, and I've been remembering what it was like when I was little; I've been remembering some of the lessons I learned about being a boy and relating to other boys, and girls, and dating, and stuff like that. I was thinking about the first time I kissed a girl, and how nervous I felt, thinking that I had done something wrong because my mom used to say that all boys had "bad thoughts" and were destined to hurt girls and women. She was really suspicious of me and was always jumping to conclusions. It really affected me having her be so negative about affection.

In this example of gentle communication about sexuality, you make it clear that you want to share your thoughts and feelings. This conversation is about you. You don't ask your partner to share his or her feelings at this time, and you don't have any spoken or unspoken wishes for mutual sharing. You make yourself vulnerable and you are creating an intimacy between yourself and your partner by being honest and open about yourself. Your partner can sense the implied permission to discuss the topic of sexuality, and he or she can also sense that there is an atmosphere of trust. This may be the first time that your partner has heard anyone talk about the subject of sexuality openly.

Because sexuality can feel like a complicated and difficult subject for discussion, it is imperative that you start very slowly, talking about your earliest thoughts and feelings about sexuality. Discussing sexuality in your childhood may trigger memories and feelings in your partner, and you can ask your partner the feelings he or she has when hearing you talk about this subject. Your partner may volunteer some information about his or her past, or may make it clear verbally or nonverbally that discussion of the subject cannot be tolerated at this time. Remember, your goal is to cultivate familiarity and comfort with open discussion of the subject of sexuality. This is the first step toward developing a positive and healthy sexual connection to complement other aspects of your relationship.

Talk About Your Understanding of Sexual Abuse

Adult survivors of sexual abuse usually feel "different" from other people. They feel stigmatized by their early experiences, and it is difficult for them to feel understood or accepted by others. Even when they are in intimate and loving relationships, there may be nagging doubts about how acceptable they are.

To help your partner with feelings of shame or low self-esteem, it is useful for you to learn all you can about sexual abuse. There are lots of books written on the subject, both by professionals and by survivors.

The books carry some basic messages, which I will summarize here. These concepts are useful to keep in mind as you interact with your spouse.

Child sexual abuse happens because the adult has a problem with sexuality and power. It is never the child's fault when he or she is sexually abused.

Children cannot stop the abuse. They may try in small or big ways that go unnoticed even to them. But the end result is the same: They don't have the physical, emotional, or mental capacity to fight off abuse by adults.

There are lots of books written on the subject.

Children don't usually tell others about abuse. They don't tell because they can't. They are afraid of being hurt, or they are afraid of the consequences of telling. Some people think kids don't tell because the abuse doesn't hurt them, or because they like it. This is not the case.

When children are sexually abused by people they love and trust, they may like the affection and attention that is given in addition to the abuse. They may therefore feel confused and guilty, and may feel "bad" because the abuse can also feel good to them.

When children are sexually abused, their bodies might

respond to being touched or caressed. Some children can later feel extremely guilty about having "liked" the abuse. Children can like being caressed and enjoy how their bodies feel when touched; this does not mean that children like being sexually abused.

Professionals who study sexuality will tell you that people make associations between sexuality and certain situations. In survivors, these associations are a result of the abuse. If a child who is sexually stimulated is always spanked, the child expects that sex will be followed by pain. These negative associations can be corrected.

As I said earlier, children who are sexually abused cannot fight back physically. They can however, fight back emotionally. One of the ways that works for children is escaping the situation mentally. Children can eventually make their bodies numb when they are being abused, or can seem to separate their minds from their bodies. Later on, any sign of sexuality can trigger this numbing-out or emotional flight, even when the adult survivor doesn't want these responses.

Children can't choose or consent to sexual abuse. Adults who sexually abuse children often think that a child seeks out sex, when in actuality they are often seeking attention or affection. In addition, some sexual offenders think that sexually abused children like the abuse because they don't say no, or fight back physically. They don't realize that sexually abused children can't fight back and don't know how to say no to adults. It's important to realize that even when children don't say "*No*" in adult terms, they also don't say "*Yes*."

Sexually abused children and adult survivors need to be believed and understood. You must make your remarks unconditional. Avoid saying things like "That is so hard to believe" or "Are you really sure that happened?" Accept that the truth is difficult for survivors to tell and those who listen must do so well.

Remember as you think about the subject of sexual abuse

as it relates to your partner, that the abuse happened to the young child, not the adult you know. You might want to look at pictures of your partner as a child so you develop an accurate mental image. It was the child who was sexually abused, and that experience tends to have far-reaching effects, particularly on his or her ability to feel relaxed or comfortable with sexual contact.

It is also possible that the person who sexually abused your partner is someone you know. For example, if the sexual abuser was someone in your partner's family, you may have ongoing contact with that person, and you may have trouble visualizing the person as an abuser. The person who sexually abused the child has also grown and developed and changed, and certainly may be a different person now. Follow your partner's lead in terms of the relationship he or she wants or needs with the offender and other extended family members.

Emphasize the Importance of Making Choices About Sex

If you were not sexually abused, you have exercised your right to choose and consent to sexual contact. You have had the experience of saying yes or no. Sexual contact has not been a terrifying proposition. It has not been experienced with fear, anxiety, and learned helplessness. Adult survivors experience sexuality in an unusual way, but their responses are appropriate to the events encountered in their childhood.

One thing most people take for granted is consent in sexual contact. Survivors will find consent an extremely unfamiliar and untrustworthy issue. They need to learn about consent slowly, experimenting with saying "No" as well as saying "Yes."

You can play an important part in this process. You can assert your respect and acceptance of your partner's ability to choose when to be sexual. Survivors will need to learn, both intellectually and emotionally, that they can lead the way.

They need to be convinced that their choices will be respected. They will need to practice saying yes and no and having those messages honored. And they will need to learn that they can change their minds and that change is also acceptable. They need to know that their voices will be heard. As your partners learn about chosen sexual contact, it is likely that their fear and anxiety will decrease. But this will not be a quick process, since their familiar feelings of fear and anxiety may resurface from time to time. Your patience and growing understanding will be helpful.

I suggest you develop a way to communicate with your partner about initiating sexual contact in a way that is safe for him or her and comfortable for you as well. You might want to ask your partner how he or she would like to be asked for sexual contact, and also find out how he or she will signal compliance or noncompliance. Be sure you discuss with your partner how to communicate that he or she has had a change of heart and no longer wants to participate in sexual contact.

If you notice that your partner is uncomfortable or appears unresponsive, talk about it.

Check in with each other periodically to see how things are going. Talk to each other and feel free to ask each other for whatever you need. If you notice that your partner is uncomfortable, or appears to be unresponsive, talk about it.

Never proceed with lovemaking if you feel unsure about your partner's participation. If the lovemaking elicits a negative response, make sure you stop and talk together about what is going on. Any and all problems experienced by adult survivors can be anticipated; appropriate and safe responses can be designed in a caring and respectful way. Share your ideas about what might help; if you are both feeling frustrated and "stuck," you may want to consult with a professional. Sexual contact between survivors and partners can evolve into a positive and more lighthearted exchange, and it will usually take some mutual attention for a period of time.

Assert the Need for Safe, Loving Sexual Contact

Survivors may find it difficult to understand and perceive sexuality as a loving or safe exchange between individuals who are mutually caring. Their experience has made them vulnerable in this area; their expectations, based on childhood experience, cause them to feel anxious anticipation. They frequently defend themselves emotionally against what they perceive to be dangerous territory. These responses are normal given their background, and yet survivors are not limited to having these responses; other responses can be developed, especially if their partners are interested in their well-being, and make efforts to produce an atmosphere of honesty, patience, and gentleness.

As a partner, you are in a position to make your intentions clear and to communicate how you perceive sexual contact and what it means to you. In other words, you can verbalize how important it is for you to make sure that sexual contact between you and your partner will be a shared experience:

You want your partner to feel safe, to feel that he or she is choosing to make love, not to make love, or to stop making love once started. You also want your partner to feel his or her body and to stay emotionally present during lovemaking. You want your partner to understand that sexual contact will not be forced. In addition, one of the important purposes for making love is to deepen the relationship of mutual love and respect. The survivor will also need to know that if he or she says "No," there are no negative or punitive consequences. Often survivors feel that if they say no, something bad will happen to them. They may expect to be punished or abandoned.

As a partner of a survivor, you may find it difficult to pay this concentrated attention to physical affection or sexuality, particularly if these areas have been comfortable to you in your life. You may feel discouraged that something you consider so normal and fun can be the source of fear and anxiety for the person you love. You may long for prior relationships in which so much work was not required. These are very common responses to this situation. It isn't easy for you either. You can end up feeling hopeless or discouraged. You may even consider leaving the relationship from time to time.

I encourage you to talk to someone about your feelings. Don't keep them bottled up. If you do, they will really interfere with your motivation about the relationship. You could begin to develop resentment toward your partner, and this resentment will probably be conveyed in one way or another. Your feelings are very important, and you need support as well.

It's helpful to keep reminding yourself that this is a temporary situation. Changes can and do occur. By making efforts toward enhancement of your relationship initially, you make an investment in your future with the person you love.

If you feel angry at your partner for not trusting you or for transferring feelings of fear to you, remember that abuse is the culprit, not your partner. Your lover was assaulted at a most vulnerable time and he or she *can* learn to view sexuality differently. The process of changing attitudes and behaviors takes time. Your patience is as crucial as your partner's. And yet patience is a difficult emotion to maintain, particularly when a few steps in the right direction can be followed by a few steps back.

Remember that you have internal and external resources. The internal resources will include affirming the overall goals of your efforts and the love you feel for your partner. You need to acknowledge and accept your feelings without being judgmental. It can be easy to scold yourself for feeling impatient, frustrated, or angry. And yet your feelings are also acceptable and must be respected. You must find productive ways of expressing your feelings and accept the fact that some days you will feel more optimistic than others. Acknowledging when you feel discouraged may have the positive side-effect of preventing a buildup of negative feelings.

Your external resources can be friends or family to whom you can turn for comfort. You don't necessarily need to confide private information, but social contact can leave you feeling warm and nurtured. If you have special friends with whom you do confide private information, you can certainly talk things through, focusing on how you are currently feeling. Ask your friend what he or she does when faced with similar feelings. It's amazing how many different ways there are of self-comfort, from being with friends, to taking walks, baking, drawing, writing, or other favorite activities.

Never underestimate the value of simply acknowledging your feelings and giving yourself permission to feel the things you do. Too frequently, individuals give themselves internal messages such as "You shouldn't feel that way" or "Snap out of it." It might be more helpful to make internal statements such as "You're having a hard time right now . . . that's okay.

Chances are things will get better soon." Or, "You have a right to your feelings. They're normal feelings to have right now. You'll be okay."

Probably the hardest aspect of confronting the difficulty of sexual contact with your partner is feeling rejected, lonely, discouraged, and impatient. Remember, it took years for your partner to develop his or her feelings, thoughts, and responses to sexuality. It will take a bulk of new experiences and a certain amount of time for small changes to take place. But they can and will.

Express Your Interest in Helping Make Sex Safe and Fun

Adult survivors find it difficult to accept the concept that sex could be fun or safe. The development of fun and safety will be accomplished with consistent, progressive positive interactions. Long, intimate talks while lying together may be a good start. One partner may want to read passages from a book to the other. Telling jokes and laughing while holding each other may also help. You may want to watch funny movies together, listen to funny audiotapes, or you may want to bring some fun games (like cards, Parcheesi, or backgammon) into bed. Some physical games that are played in the bedroom can also begin to create new associations between physical intimacy and good sensations. Games that require nonsexual touching are good, such as the one I mentioned earlier where two persons join hands and take turns leading the motion. Couples can also have fun feeding each other or licking sticky materials (such as peanut butter, jelly, or whipped cream) from each other's fingers. It's important to keep a constant vigil on your partner's reactions. Any sign of discomfort or spacing out will trigger the need to stop immediately without asking why, and without pressure to continue the behavior.

Talk About Initiating Sex

All couples will need to design methods of signaling interest in sexual contact. It's important to practice asking for love-making and answering requests from partners. Some of the signals are verbal and some are not. The messages need to be as clear as possible, and they need to be understood. Otherwise there is danger that the signals will not be received or reciprocated and either one or both of you can develop resentment based on assumptions of rejection.

One couple I knew came to therapy because they were not having sex as often as they both wanted. They were very clear that each wanted to have sex at least twice a month, yet they found that sometimes months passed without any contact. One of the partners, Jim, had been sexually abused by a mother who had constantly demanded his speedy performance. He felt insecure in his ability to please his wife since he could never satisfy his mother. Jim's wife, Marie, was very sympathetic and yet she felt uncertain about how to ask for lovemaking. She felt that Jim was a gentle and caring lover and she looked forward to their lovemaking. For his part, Jim was afraid to ask Marie to make love, assuming that he would be rejected for his unskillful lovemaking. It was positive that each person could share his or her vulnerability about lovemaking. It was clear that to be of assistance I would need to help them deal with stubborn insecurities and fears and at the same time give them communication skills so they could more successfully have their needs met. The therapy was very brief, and once their communication resulted in more frequent lovemaking, both individuals felt more secure and confident about performance and desirability.

Jim and Marie took turns asking the other to make love. Jim liked to ask verbally and he gently stated, "Honey, I would love it if we could make love together." Marie loved being asked, and although we had discussed how she might say no if she was not interested, she did not anticipate that particular problem coming up too frequently. Marie preferred nonverbal communication, and she would usually caress her husband to signal her interest in lovemaking. Apparently Jim had not previously understood that caressing signaled interest in sexuality since sometimes he found the caressing nurturing and would fall asleep. Jim and Marie naturally came to the conclusion that there were times they wanted hugging and caressing but not necessarily lovemaking. In these instances they had devised yet another signal.

Talk About How to Stop Sex Once Started

As I mentioned earlier, the question of choice is very important for adult survivors. They need to choose when and if they want to have sexual contact, and they need to have the option of changing their minds. They may think they are willing to make love at any given time, and yet a number of difficulties may suddenly arise along with the need to stop lovemaking midstream.

Stopping sex once it has started is not an easy task for either party. Once sexual momentum starts, it is frustrating and difficult to change gears. And yet the option to do so must exist if your partner is to feel safe and truly free to choose sexual contact.

You must make an unconditional commitment to stop if asked to do so. Your response must be immediate and decisive. You will need to consider what you will do should this happen, and it is useful if you talk with your partner about what you may do and what your partner may do if lovemaking is abruptly interrupted. You may need to leave the room for a while. You may need to express some frustration. But the message you give must be clear: "This is hard for me right now, but you have a right to ask me to stop, and I want to respect that. It's important for me that you can ask, because that way we can be sure of each other." Your partner likewise may need to leave the room, or regroup in some way. Chances are that he or she has asked you to stop because some frightening feeling has surfaced suddenly. Your partner may need some time alone, or may even need to be held and reassured. Try to talk ahead of time about what you can anticipate, but also talk together afterward to find out how the situation could have been handled differently. Any difficult situation will be greatly helped by keeping the lines of communication open. If words cannot be exchanged, perhaps you and your partner can write down your thoughts and exchange notes when appropriate. Probably the most important thing to keep in mind is that your partner is asking you to stop because he or she trusts you enough to do so and because you are working together on improving your relationship.

Talk About Likes and Dislikes

Everyone has specific likes and dislikes regarding foreplay and sexual contact. It is very important for adult survivors to recognize and acknowledge preferences. Initially, survivors may be more aware of what is disliked than what is liked. It is only after a certain degree of comfort with sexuality and lovemaking that positive preferences can be experienced and discovered.

Everything that has been discussed so far will help create an atmosphere of honesty, safety, and trust. This atmosphere is necessary for the continued development of quality contact between lovers.

Talk About Triggers

"Triggers" are sounds, sights, smells, sensations, noises, or other stimuli that can cause unexpected emotional responses in adult survivors. Janice was an adult survivor of sexual abuse who had forgotten her early abusive experiences for many years. In her twenties she entered into a sexual relationship. When she smelled liquor on her partner's breath, she was triggered to remember her sexual abuse. As a result of the memory she became frightened and ran away from her lover, breaking off their relationship. It was months before she was able to understand what had happened and only then was she able to seek therapy for survivor issues.

Triggers may be unknown to adult survivors, and the more emotionally present survivors are during lovemaking, the greater the likelihood that external triggers can set off unforeseen emotional responses.

It is possible that the time of day or night, the location, the temperature, the way a survivor is touched, words spoken, physical positions, or types of caress may trigger unpleasant responses in survivors. It is critical for partners of survivors to understand the occurrence of these triggers and know how to respond. Survivors need to talk about the triggers they have experienced and about what their partners can do to help. It is usually helpful when your partner gets triggered to say clearly and repeatedly, "You're safe now. This is me. I'm not going to hurt you or take advantage of you. That happened in the past. I know you feel scared or confused. That's okay. I love you and I want you to have your feelings and to know that you are now safe." This kind of reassurance can be very effective.

Talk About Dissociation

As I've discussed earlier, everyone can dissociate and therefore you are probably familiar with the experience of "spacing out" on a temporary basis.

Become aware of your partner and of what he or she looks like when dissociating. Talk together about how to respond. There may be times when you simply notice that your partner is not emotionally available and you wait until he or she comes back. There are other times that you may want to help your partner be present: "Honey, you've gone away. I need you to be here with me." Simple statements like this may or may not work. Your partner may require a touch on the hand or a hug accompanied by the statement. Your partner, of course, has a right to decline; he or she may need to take some time alone and you need to respect the process.*

When making love, it's probably important for you to know that your partner is with you. This is not a time you want to feel alone. If your partner gets a flashback, becomes frightened, or dissociates, it's important to stop and see what's going on. A good rule of thumb is to stop as soon as you can see that your partner has left emotionally. Talk to him or her and offer reassurance and comfort. It will often be possible to resume lovemaking once your partner is available. To make love when your partner is dissociative is counterproductive. Difficult as it may be to have your lovemaking interrupted, you need to be attentive to your partner and understand that he or she uses these responses to stay as safe as possible. You will become more and more safe and trustworthy in your partner's eyes if you remain consistent in your kind and respectful responses and approach your partner with dignity and tenderness.

---

*Sometimes survivors of severe childhood abuse dissociate and appear to become a different person, speaking in a childlike voice, or relating to you in a new way. Your partner may have a condition called "multiple personalities" and if this is the case, it will help both of you to get a consultation, diagnosis, and assistance from a professional who specializes in this area. Multiplicity is not a sign of mental illness—it is a remarkable way in which children defend themselves against horrendous and painful abuse.

Chapter 4

POWER AND CONTROL
A Balanced Distribution

I try to make sure she has a say in everything we do together, but sometimes she goes along with me, probably because she's scared to disagree. Later it comes out that she really didn't want to do something and then I end up feeling like the bad guy. I hate it that she can't trust that when I ask her what she wants to do, I really mean it. This has got to be the worst of our problems. She's scared all the time and I end up feeling like a big, bad ogre.

Abused children have limited ways of defending themselves against abuse. Older youngsters may be able to run away or devise ways of being relocated to safer environments. Younger children don't have the capacity to escape physically and seem to employ psychological ways of escaping emotionally or avoiding or postponing the feelings of pain, sorrow, fear, or anger.

Another common and effective way that children protect themselves from abuse in or outside their families is to convey full and unequivocal compliance. In other words, they feel and behave in a helpless manner in an attempt to avoid further physical or emotional assaults.

Children at risk develop survival mechanisms to thwart the original danger. However, when the threat no longer persists, the behavior that was once prudent can become an obstacle to survival.

Learned helplessness and compliance are helpful and frequently effective. Abused children do what they are told and they make few demands. They seem to "blend into the woodwork," eliciting minimal attention from others.

These children have little spontaneity or playfulness. They take few risks in any area, lack curiosity, and remain understimulated. They show little emotion and may be isolated from peers. They may, however, devote themselves to study, achieving well academically. They may also find a sport and develop physical strength or mastery. These children may get little attention from teachers because they require little direction or discipline. They become self-sufficient in an adultlike way. They establish a way to stay safe from danger, but unfortunately, in doing so they also screen out pleasant or rewarding exchanges. This isolation is quite a burden for these children. They should be receiving care, attention, and nurturing. Instead, they must protect themselves from contact with others who are perceived as being unsafe and unrewarding.

One obvious effect of abuse on the survivors is a feeling of powerlessness. The larger, stronger abuser dominates the smaller, weaker child. There is little opportunity for a child who experiences abuse in any form to learn about his or her own power, or how to have a healthy balance of power with others.

Children usually learn about balance of power through their experiences with adults and peers, but as we have seen, abused children are ill-prepared to have normal exchanges with anyone, including other children. They tend to withdraw from others, and therefore the usual range of interactions is never fully explored.

Personal power is a broad concept that includes the ability to speak, ask, negotiate, invite, demand, resolve conflicts, get attention, and develop feelings of safety, adequacy, self-control, and self-esteem. The individual who feels personal power enters an interaction in a grounded way; he or she feels on equal footing with others. The individual who feels personal power is not overwhelmed with anxious feelings and feels **entitled** to respect and thoughtfulness from others. These can be areas we take for granted if we grew up in environments that nurtured and protected our right to be safe. But children who are raised in atmospheres of violence, inappropriate sexuality, or emotional abuse or neglect are children who must divert all their energies to the task of surviving from day to day. They cannot acquire skills that come naturally to other children. These abused children enter adulthood with clear vulnerabilities and underdeveloped areas that have remained unexplored. The hope is that these important areas can be explored within the context of a safe adult relationship where the basic issue of safety can be taken for granted, creating a safe place for investigation of other aspects of the relationship. Adult survivors must feel the internal and external safety to go out on "scouting expeditions" so as to better understand and establish equality in their important relationships.

As partners of adult survivors you may enter the relationship with feelings of respect and love. You may be not only willing but able to provide your partner with opportunities for balanced and loving exchanges of power. You want the relationship to feel equal to both of you.

You may find yourself wanting your partner to make choices or decisions in his or her life, or you may be very sensitive about not imposing your opinions on him or her. You may feel uncertain about how to proceed, recognizing this as an emotional and yet momentous aspect of the relationship.

I offer the following suggestions for working on this aspect of the relationship:

- Define the subject together
- Talk about what each of you would like
- Talk about your worst fears
- Rehearse exchanges of power
- Practice balancing power
- Discuss what to do when either person changes opinion
- Think about creating internal/external safety

Define the Subject Together

The subject of power and the balance of power in your relationship must be discussed. It's important for you to take the lead and introduce the subject in a manner consistent with your goal. For example, you might tender your hopes in this way:

I've been thinking about our relationship and how much I enjoy us being together. I think that there are some things I'd like to talk about to make sure they are as okay for you as they are for me. One of those is how we go about sharing power in our relationship. I want us to have equality so most of the time we make decisions together. I want to make sure you feel safe enough to voice your opinions because I respect your thoughts and I want you to feel comfortable to disagree or agree with me. And other times I want us to be able to make decisions alone and the other person can agree, or even disagree, and have that be okay too. I thought we could just talk about it for a while.

One way that power is exerted in a relationship is by the decisions made within the relationship. Obviously, joint decisions are probably the most effective, but there will be times when decisions are made by you or your partner, and individuals in a healthy relationship will find room for making both individual and collective decisions. Inherent in the decision-making process is the ability to communicate openly with mutual respect for each other's point of view. The ability to negotiate is an important part of communication.

In the example above, you are conveying a number of important central ideas as well as your willingness to talk about improving and enhancing the relationship. You may want to write down the message for your partner and let him or her read it and digest it quietly, before talking about it further. Sometimes when specific areas are "charged," that is, if they immediately bring up strong emotions, it takes some time to process them and understand the thoughts associated with these strong feelings. One adult survivor would report back to me, "When I heard the word 'power' I immediately cringed physically and I could feel my heart pounding and my hands become sweaty. I couldn't hear anything else that he was saying to me. It took me quite a while before my body slowed down enough for me to think through what he was saying and that it wasn't something bad." She went on to say, "I've never been with somebody who was in the least interested in what I think or feel. When Sam asks, it still throws me for a loop, but after four years I'm beginning to believe that not only does he want to know, but sometimes he wants me to **volunteer** this information without being asked. That's really tough!"

Talk About What Each of You Would Like

Once you have an agreement to proceed talking about this area of your relationship, you can begin by telling your spouse what you would like to see happen, and then listening to his or her views about personal power.

Prepare your thoughts on the subject beforehand and be sure you have some specificity to share. Again, practicing or rehearsing can be valuable. The more you can describe what you want from your partner and yourself in terms of behavior, the better. This way, an area that is already unfamiliar and vague can begin to take shape in your partner's mind. For example, "I want you to participate more in decisions" is vague. What does it mean? Participate how? Instead, the following statement gives specifics: "I'd like us to sit down together to talk when we have an important decision to make. I'd like to hear what you think and I'd like you to hear my thoughts. Then I'd like us to talk together about both points of view and come to a conclusion about what's best. Sometimes I think I say too much. I want you to tell me more about your thoughts and I want us to take the same amount of time when we speak." As a matter of fact, couples often use timers to ensure that both individuals are getting equal time. Although using timers may feel superficial and contrived at first, they can also symbolize a mutual interest in establishing positive patterns, particularly when previous (problematic or dissatisfying) patterns have been identified.

It may be difficult for your partner to tell you clearly what is wanted because he or she may not be able to visualize a desired outcome. If this is the case, you may want to create a scenario and help your partner "walk through it" with you. If you choose to do this, make sure you choose an area that is not threatening in the sense that it's something you haven't recently quarreled about, or a scenario that is too unrealistic to imagine.

Talk About Your Worst Fears

I believe it is always helpful to dispel fears by verbalizing them. Some fears of adult survivors seem unrealistic and/or inconceivable to their partners. Here's an example of a communication between an adult survivor and her partner that was *not* effective:

LAURA: Why are you just sitting there? Answer me!
SANDY: Don't scream at me.
LAURA: I'm not screaming. I'm frustrated. I want you to answer me.
SANDY: I can't.
LAURA: Why not? You act like you think I'm gonna hurt you or something.
SANDY: I do think that.
LAURA: Give me a break. When have I ever hurt you in any way? I'm sick and tired of your cowering. When are you gonna grow up and quit expecting people to hurt you. I'll tell you what. It's effective. There's nothing I can do when you get this way. . . .

It's important to note that this partner's feelings of frustration and anger are understandable. The partner in this example, Laura, felt very helpless and hurt. She had been in a relationship with her lover Sandy for eight years. They had been unable to resolve most conflicts because Sandy would always cower and withdraw into a silence. Laura said that she had made many efforts to make her lover feel safe. She was totally nonviolent and would never threaten her or hurt her in any way. Laura felt that Sandy's responses were directed toward her own physically abusive father and she was now paying the price. Laura's anger toward Sandy's father had become huge, and yet she felt she had no outlet for this anger. She was also angry with Sandy's recoiling behavior, which had become a way for Sandra to avoid settling any arguments between them. My suggestion to this couple resulted in the following more effective communication:

SANDY: Don't yell at me.

LAURA: I'll keep my voice more quiet. I really want us to work this out together. Sandra, tell me something. When my voice gets loud, what do you think will happen next?

SANDY: I don't know.

LAURA: Try to think about it. When my voice is loud, what do you think I'll do next?

SANDY: I think you're gonna hit me.

Now instead of saying "Give me a break," or "Have I ever hit you?" Laura says,

I'm sorry you feel scared. I know that when people yelled at you they usually hit you. I will keep my voice down, and look, I will sit over here, sitting on my hands, and I promise you I won't get loud, or stand up, or hit you. I'm Laura, not your mom or dad. I don't hit people, and I won't hit you. I love you and I will never hurt you on purpose.

As you can see, Sandy and Laura are now in a position to talk together about the problem they are having. It's not that this reassurance alone is going to create an immediate and full change in Sandy's behavior, but it is the only way Sandy will begin to have new experiences. As these experiences become more and more familiar, and Sandy begins to trust them, she will probably be better able to "stay with" whatever is going on rather than feel overwhelmed and cowering.

Laura felt better as soon as she learned to respond in this way because it made her feel less helpless. She had a technique for responding, and she could see that Sandy responded well to being reassured. Again, reassurances alone do not suffice. These new experiences need to be felt intellectually and emotionally. Partners need to feel that others are patient and will persevere. Patience and perseverance do pay off.

Be sure that you reciprocate with your own fears and worries. Everyone has a few, and it's important to share them so that survivors don't feel themselves to be freaks but rather people with workable problems. Share your fears and worries honestly. If you make things up your partner will probably detect dishonesty easily and quickly.

Rehearse Exchanges of Power

One of the best ways to address fears and worries is through a process called "desensitization," in which the feared object or situation is slowly and methodically approached. For example, if an individual is frightened of dogs, he or she may first look at a still picture of a dog, then listen to an audio of a dog's bark, then watch a video of a dog, then walk with someone by a dog penned in a fenced area, then pet a small puppy, then eventually walk alone past the fenced area, then perhaps pet a small and docile full-grown dog. The idea is that the individual faces his or her fears in small increments, learning to tolerate anxiety while developing coping strategies for the uncomfortable feeling. In addition, the new and safe experiences with animals can combat previous negative associations.

The topic of power in a relationship can be frightening and anxiety-provoking for adult survivors. It will almost always be helpful to practice or rehearse exchanges of power particularly about nonthreatening issues.

Select some issues between the two of you that both of you perceive as innocent. An example of this might be cooking a meal. You and your partner can make a decision about a day of the week when each can be responsible for making the decisions and the preparations. I caution here that this should be done only if cooking and eating is not a sensitive subject.

Another idea might be to select a day of the week to go out as a couple. Make the decision ahead of time about who will be picking out the activity for the evening. Brainstorm together about the types of activities that can be selected. This might help each partner have a notion of the possible range of activities and selections.

The purpose of this exercise is for survivor-partners to have an opportunity to experiment with their personal power in a safe and structured way. The survivor will have firsthand knowledge of what it is like to choose, to propose his or her ideas, and to experience what it's like to have personal power.

As the survivor becomes more trusting and confident, the couple can progress to exchanges of power in other more important areas such as how money is spent, where one lives, work, vacation, sexual contact, and so on.

Practice Balancing Power

As you do the above exercises, keep an eye on balance and equality. Couples need to feel an equality in their relationship. This creates a feeling of affiliation and respect. Even if one partner is more or less comfortable with personal power, the couple should monitor the distribution of tasks so that a comfortable balance is maintained.

Couples can make a list of household chores, partners choosing the chores they prefer, leaving the unchosen areas to be equally distributed and rotated.

Let's hypothesize that a typical "list" will include things like paying bills, dropping off or picking up children, cleaning the kitchen, washing clothes, feeding a pet, and grocery shopping. Each partner selects preferred duties and what's left is divided equally. This sharing of responsibilities will institute a sense of mutuality between partners; mutuality goes a long way to encourage a shared contentment in the relationship.

Discuss What to Do When Either Person Changes Opinion

So far, we've looked at ways in which individuals can make decisions and experiment with a feeling of balanced power in the relationship. Equally important is to anticipate the possibility of an individual's changing his or her mind. Everyone has a right to have a change of opinion, and there should be room in a relationship for this to occur. Someone who can shift from one idea to another is practicing personal power, although it can be uncomfortable for the other person to adjust to the change.

In order to achieve a sense of personal power and control, an individual must constantly acknowledge his or her thoughts and feelings and, based on new information, make desired or necessary alterations.

Think About Creating Internal/External Safety

This is an important topic not only when discussing power, but in almost any other aspect of the relationship. Survivors are acutely sensitive to feeling unsafe and vulnerable, and you can make efforts to contribute to your partner's feeling of security. This subject is discussed at length in the following chapter.

Chapter 5

SAFETY

Making the World a Safe Place

It breaks my heart when I see her flinch or cower. I try so hard to make her feel comfortable and safe, but sometimes I despair. I think sometimes the best thing is to leave her alone; at least alone she's not afraid. The problem is when I leave her alone, I feel like we're growing further apart. I don't know what to do.

Abused, neglected, or traumatized children are terrorized at a time when they are ill-equipped to cope with such strong feelings. If their environment remains painful, hurt children cannot heal and learn from new, positive experiences. They begin to view the world as unsafe and are mistrustful of interactions with people or of new situations. All people may be seen as threatening because people have been hurtful, inconsistent, or unrewarding in the past. New situations bring challenges that require social skills; survivors of abuse often feel inadequate in these situations.

Many survivors continue to live in the emotional climate of the abuse or trauma throughout their adult lives. What this means is that no matter what changes have occurred, survivors still have the emotional responses that arose in reaction to their original traumatic situations. Adult survivors can feel cautious, reticent, or emotionally paralyzed, and suffer from strong feelings of helplessness and a desire to withdraw into the safety of isolation.

It is true that you cannot alter the survivor's internal experience. He or she will need to find ways of developing a sense of safety and security.

You do, however, play an important role. You can make an important **contribution** to your partner's sense of well-being. There are definite ways in which you can assist in devising an approach that encourages the development of an emotional sanctuary:

- Talk about feelings of safety
- Be responsive to requests by your partner
- Volunteer to cooperate
- Let your partner know you understand

Talk About Feelings of Safety

As I've emphasized throughout this book, adult survivors struggle to obtain a feeling of safety and security, particularly within an intimate relationship, where the greatest threat is perceived. You can be helpful by talking about times in your life when you felt uncertain or frightened. It will probably help your partner a great deal simply to listen to your description of shared experiences and feelings. You may or may not have been hurt as a child by your parents, but chances are you can think of childhood events that made you feel threatened, helpless, hopeless, or trapped.

Talk about current fears, concerns, and worries as well. Search within yourself for situations that produce these responses and tell your partner. Many survivors feel ashamed of their feelings and may benefit from seeing that such feelings are experienced by other adults.

Be sure you talk a little about what makes you feel more safe and secure after you've described an unsettling situation for yourself. By sharing this information you may be giving your partner some ideas about additional coping strategies.

Be Responsive to Requests by Your Partner

Your partner may have a number of strategies that help him or her feel safer. Be sure that you let your partner know that any and all ways that increase safety are acceptable and desirable.

Some survivors like to hold and hug stuffed animals. These may have been companions in childhood. Holding on to a stuffed animal during a difficult conversation or situation can make a great deal of difference. Other strategies for safety that I have seen used by survivors include sitting on the floor to have a conversation, writing things down and letting someone read the letter prior to discussion, going outdoors, having background music, talking to friends on the phone, and the like. Make sure you are receptive, nonjudgmental, and compassionate. As your partner trusts you more and more, fewer coping strategies will be needed.

Volunteer to Cooperate

Let your partner know that you are interested and willing to do whatever you can to help him or her with feelings of safety. Beyond that, volunteer to experiment with new ways of interacting to see if something helps. Ask your partner if there is something you can do or say to help with feelings of safety.

Let Your Partner Know You Understand

Be sure you reassure your partner as you observe his or her coping strategies. Don't ask why he or she feels threatened or worried. Don't be impatient or harsh. Follow your partner's lead. You can't convince survivors to feel safer, they must find the sense of safety for themselves.

Chapter 6

COMMUNICATION
The Deep Freeze or Verbal Spillage

No matter what we do, we can't figure out how to talk to each other without bringing out the big guns. We get nowhere in a hurry. We start calling each other names and bringing up every little thing that we've done to hurt each other. It's so frustrating. We end up with one of us crying, and it's gotten so that we are scared to say anything to each other.

Communication has long been recognized by marital counselors as one of the most important contributors in making or breaking a relationship. If the lines of communication are open, any problem can be addressed. If partners know how to talk with each other and how to listen, the possibility of identifying and resolving conflicts through negotiation and compromise is highly increased. Contrary to what many people believe, all healthy relationships include conflict; the challenge lies in developing approaches to confronting and resolving them.

Survivors of childhood abuse come from families with varying degrees of problematic behaviors. Almost all abusive families have great deficits in communication, either using an accusatory, punitive, and hurtful style of communicating or using silence, which can communicate uninterest, anger, disappointment, or emotional disconnectedness. Survivors were not encouraged to recognize or share their thoughts and feelings. They did not observe reasonable and effective communication. They may have been punished for talking or asking questions. They may have been threatened to stay quiet; being silent may have kept them safe from unwanted punitive attention. Positive communication skills were never taught. Abused children did not have the opportunity to benefit from firsthand observation of effective communication.

Luckily, some abused children learn about communication in other settings and from individuals who give them the attention and support they need. Sometimes children are able to take risks in these new and rewarding environments, and they may experiment with open communication. Other children find it difficult to become comfortable with these new forms of encouragement and may be unable to experiment freely.

In order to create an atmosphere of safety in which positive communication can occur, and in order to have rewarding exchanges that will promote the usefulness of healthy communication, both partners in a relationship need to develop and manage their communication with certain basic principles in mind.

- Select the proper time and place to communicate
- Structure the exchange as you wish
- Use "I" messages
- Begin with positive statements
- Respond to signs of discomfort or concern in your partner
- Be concrete, avoid vague or abstract concepts

- Stay in the present
- Say what you want and what you are willing to do
- Listen to your partner and reiterate what you hear
- Find areas for negotiation
- Agree to disagree
- Practice
- Follow up on agreements

Select the Proper Time and Place to Communicate

Be sure to make careful choices about how and when to approach your partner for a talk. If he or she has recently been triggered, and appears to be experiencing emotional distress, wait for a better time. You want to be supportive and helpful when your partner is in distress, but this will not necessarily be the best time to communicate. You might gently say, "I want to hold you and be here for you right now, and maybe later we can talk about what was upsetting." If your partner wants to share some thoughts now, simply listen and be reassuring. You can always reintroduce the subject at a later time.

If your partner has become extremely angry about something and he or she needs time to calm down, respect the request, and try to discuss the concern at a later time.

If your partner is finding it hard to "stay present" and you observe that he or she is spacing out, wait until a better time to try to talk. Paying attention to the emotional availability and receptivity of your partner will go a long way in securing a successful exchange.

Likewise, try to select an environment that will be conducive to talking. Make sure the environment is comfortable, both in terms of room temperature and in terms of physical comfort. There is nothing worse than trying to be sensitive and reassuring to someone when your hands and feet are freezing, or you are sitting in a chair that hurts your back.

Decide together about a comfortable environment and try different things. Some people like to go out rather than stay at home; a talk in a restaurant over dinner or a walk in the park may be inspiring to some.

Ask ahead of time so your partner feels as if he or she has a choice. For example, "Nick, I'd like to talk with you some-time today. Would you let me know when's a good time for you?" may be a better approach than saying "Nick, I've been waiting all day to talk to you. Can we talk now?" In the latter situation, the person who wants to talk will feel anxious about finding "the right time" and may develop resentments over having to wait for someone else to appear available. At the same time, if you are the one being approached, this may not be the best time for you, and yet hearing that your

A talk in a restaurant or a walk . . .

partner has been waiting for you all day, you may feel obligated to make time to listen. Feelings of obligation are not usually helpful to effective communication.

If you and your partner make talking a regular part of your relationship, it is less likely that either will feel frightened or anxious when a request for a conversation is made. The less you do talk however, the more likely you are to feel worried or "put on notice" when your partner asks for some time to talk. This is reminiscent of being a child in school and having the principal ask you to come to his or her office. The first thought was usually, "Oh, oh. I'm in trouble now." To avoid feeling such concern when either you or your partner want to talk, the best advice is to make talking a regular habit.

Structure the Exchange as You Wish

There are lots of ways you can approach a talk. Some of them will feel more difficult than others. Make sure you and your partner have specific ways to signal whether the talk is difficult or easy.

Here's how Jack and Charlie worked it out.

Jack had become very worried about his inability to communicate with Charlie. Charlie had been physically abused as a child and had strong feelings of inadequacy. He believed it was his fault that he was abused by his father. Charlie insisted the abuse was his fault and that his dad was just trying to teach him and mold him into a stronger person. He was extremely sensitive to anyone talking to him because the only time his father paid attention to him was when he chastised Charlie for some perceived wrongdoing.

Jack complained that when he tried to talk to Charlie about anything, Charlie cowered and became emotionally remote. Jack feared their relationship was at risk because there was no talking between them at all.

Jack decided that the only way to break through this pattern of avoidance was to structure the talks into categories. Jack would talk about himself and his work, his childhood, current activities, philosophical or political topics, aspects of the relationship that were working well, and problems in the relationship. He would ask Charlie for a time to talk, stating clearly the topic he wanted to discuss. He would always present nonthreatening subjects before moving to the most difficult subject, namely, the problems in the relationship.

Charlie was reluctant at first, but his greatest fear was losing this relationship with Jack, which meant so much to him. He agreed reluctantly and found that it was actually fun and interesting to listen to Jack talk about himself, his values, his political and philosophical views, and so on. He particularly liked hearing about the facets of their relationship that made Jack content.

By the time the talk came around to problems in the relationship, Charlie had some firsthand experience with communication. He had listened to Jack in the past, and had actually felt compelled to share his own views about different topics. There was some experience to draw from.

Jack selected an easy problem between them for the first talk and asked Charlie to cooperate in a specific manner. Charlie had been surprised by the outcome and this experience made it easier for the couple to tackle more difficult subjects later on.

In addition, another way to structure a talk might be to set a time frame, and to state the topic and the difficulty level ahead of time. For example, you may want to start out by saying, "I'd like us to talk about money and how to prioritize paying the bills this month. It will probably take a couple of hours to do this, and I want you to know I feel really worried about talking with you about this." As you can see, the topic is defined to avoid the anxiety that someone can feel waiting to hear what the talk is about, there is a time frame for the discussion, and the degree of difficulty has been defined.

When you hear an approach like this, you can respond in kind. "I know this is a hard topic for us to discuss, but I'm glad you're bringing it up. We do need to put our heads together to make some good decisions about our money. If it's going to take a couple of hours, let me grab a sandwich first."

Make sure your partner knows the degree of difficulty involved in the talk you're about to have. If necessary, ask your partner to hold his or her comments until you are finished. When it's difficult to bring something up, it will help if there are no interruptions.

As you can see, communicating can be difficult, but difficulties can be faced as long as you focus on developing strategies that result in achieving your goal: to talk together, resolve conflicts, and strengthen your relationship.

Use "I" Messages

One of the fundamental rules of good communication during arguments is to make "I" statements rather than talk about the other person. This rule will almost always have positive results since you will always be on safe territory: you will be talking about something you know.

Let me illustrate this point in the following example.

Tony and Jennifer felt extremely frustrated by attempts to communicate about even the simplest things. Jennifer had an emotionally abusive parent who had belittled and criticized her harshly all her life. While she was unable to stand up to her father, she was adamant about standing up to anyone else who attempted to belittle her in any way. The problem for this couple was that Tony's communication style aggravated Jennifer's vulnerability and Jennifer's responses angered Tony. This couple escalated any communication into an argument with no resolution. See how quickly the couple become irritated and upset with each other.

TONY: Jenny, you make me crazy! I'm not going to put up with this anymore. You need to fix this right away. You screwed up the bills again.

JENNIFER: Yes, sir, I'll be there right away, sir. Heaven forbid I should be late when Your Majesty calls.

TONY: Cut it out, Jennifer. You know darn well that we can't go on with you bouncing checks like crazy. We're supporting the bank with all your penalty fees. You must like all the attention you get from them.

JENNIFER: You are full of it, Tony. I haven't bounced a check in months.

TONY: What do you call this?

JENNIFER: That's the first one I've bounced in months.

TONY: That's what you say every time and I'm sick of it. Any fourth-grader has the math to balance a checkbook. How did you manage to get through high school?

JENNIFER: Oh, excuse me, Mr. Einstein. I forgot that you, of course, are superior in every way. I'll tell you what. You balance the checkbook from now on. I'm going to open my own account and we won't have this argument anymore.

TONY: That's no solution. What are you talking about? Two accounts won't work. Jenny, get back here, you spoiled little brat.

JENNIFER: I'm out of here. You don't want little brats hanging around, do you?

This was typical of the communication problem between Jennifer and Tony, and as you can see, it was totally unproductive. Both of them ended up feeling depressed, frustrated, angry, and hopeless. These feelings were not hard to understand given the fact that nothing had been resolved, and the tension between them had increased.

There are many ways that this communication could be

improved, and this important topic could be addressed. For example, instead of Tony's opening statement, a better way to approach Jennifer might be to say, "Jenny, you've been doing really well lately about not bouncing checks, but I've got some bad news, we just got a notice from the bank." Tony could then go on to say, "I'm really worried about our finances and I need your help to figure things out. Can you spare some time today so we can talk about our checking account? I'd really like us to put our heads together and figure out a helpful solution." Now Tony is nonaccusatory and, as a matter of fact, compliments Jennifer about how well she's been doing on the checking account. His urgency for discussing this matter is clearly communicated without sounding demanding and authoritative. He is making an effort to convey the notion that balancing the checkbook is an issue that both partners must address together. Jennifer will probably feel less defensive and therefore more willing to cooperate. Tony will feel more willing to proceed if he believes his partner is willing to work on the problem with him.

Accusations and belittling statements are never helpful since they are hurtful and usually elicit a retaliatory response.

Avoid statements that begin with "You." In the above dialogue the most hurtful statements are "you make me crazy," "you've screwed up," "you fix this," "how did you get through high school," and "you spoiled little brat." These statements are accusatory and critical. They do little to encourage open dialogue.

More helpful statements are "I am worried about our finances," "I need your help," and "I'd like us to put our heads together and figure out a helpful solution."

Also remember to talk about your feelings and not your partner's feelings. Your feelings are important too. Don't use "I" messages in a negative way. For example, "I'm sick and tired of your screwups" is not a positive or respectful statement even though it begins with "I." Likewise, "I feel like you're not listening" manages to carry an indictment, even though it starts with "I." Notice how the meaning changes when you say, "I feel unheard. What I have to say is important and I want to make sure you're listening." In this last statement you're talking only about yourself rather than something the other person is or isn't doing.

Begin with Positive Statements

I've been promoting the use of positive statements throughout this book because everyone likes to be validated and everyone will respond more favorably to a positive statement than to a negative or accusatory one.

At the same time, it is important to remember that adult survivors may feel uncomfortable with positive statements, and yet they need to develop a tolerance for them. I encourage you, therefore, to practice making random positive statements; do not limit your positive statements to times when you are going to introduce a request for discussion.

In the preceding example, Tony complimented Jennifer on how well she had been doing with her checking account in the recent past. This statement allowed Jennifer to feel supported, and she could therefore feel more receptive to listening further.

Respond to Signs of Discomfort or Concern in Your Partner

Some adult survivors will have a flight response to any attempts on your part to discuss difficult subjects. Your survivor partner may feel uncomfortable, afraid, inadequate, or hopeless. Be sure that you proceed with caution and check in with your partner, reassuring him or her that this is a safe discussion, with no hitting, and that you are not angry. You might also ask if there is anything you can do that would make your partner feel safer. Often, survivors will be able to direct you accordingly and may make simple requests that will allow them increased feelings of security.

Be Concrete, Avoid Vague or Abstract Concepts

Another pitfall in communication occurs when terms are used that are vague or obscure and that lead to misunderstandings. Be sure you maximize your chances of being understood by **describing** something (behaviorally if possible), rather than using words or phrases that are subject to interpretation. Here are a few examples that will clarify these differences in meaning.

Maria turns to her lover Stan and says, "I feel really down today. . . . Could you spend some time with me and help me cheer up?" Stan is sympathetic but feels immediately pressured to do something to help. The pressure mounts as some of his efforts go unnoticed, and eventually he gives up trying. Maria now feels as though she has asked and her request has been ignored. Stan ends up feeling inadequate and unappreciated. Both the request for assistance and the desire to be of assistance are worthwhile efforts; the inability to communicate more clearly creates ambiguity and pressure to perform. Instead, Maria could ask for attention in the following way: "Stan, I feel really down today. I'd really appreciate some support from you. Would you mind running a bath for me and taking me out to dinner and a movie?" Along the same lines, Maria might want to ask for physical attention: "Stan, I'm feeling really down right now. Could we lie down together and listen to music? I would really like to feel your arms around me. I know that cuddling for a while will cheer me up." In both these examples, Stan has a much better idea what to do and the pressure to perform decreases immediately.

If Maria could not come up with a specific idea, perhaps she and Stan could spend some time talking about what might help cheer her up. Both of them can suggest things that have worked in the past. In this way, Stan's pressure to come up with an effective form of reassurance will decrease, and Maria can steer him away from activities that will not help her at all.

Stay in the Present

Another extremely important rule of communication is to stay in the present. There may be a temptation to bring up old resentments or to try to tackle more than one concern at a time. Past events with associated unresolved feelings will contaminate a couple's ability to negotiate a current conflict. Some people call these old feelings regarding past unresolved events "extra luggage" that individuals carry around. This luggage weighs people down and causes them to feel burdened or hopeless.

Watch how quickly this communication deteriorates between Lisa and Tony.

LISA: I just don't understand why you can't call when you're going to be late.

TONY: I was busy . . . there wasn't a phone around. I thought if I stopped to call, I would just get home later.

LISA: That would be much better than not calling at all.

TONY: Okay, okay. Next time I promise I'll call you no matter what.

LISA: That's what you said last time.

TONY: What do you want from me? It's over now. I'm sorry, okay?

LISA: Yeah, you were sorry two years ago when we missed our plane to Hawaii, and you were sorry when we missed the awards dinner, and of course you're sorry each and every time we go into a movie ten or fifteen minutes late and miss the beginning.

TONY: Well, I am sorry. I don't understand why this is such a big deal to you. It's not like you've never been late.

LISA: When have I been late and not called you?

TONY: I guess you're perfect. . . .

LISA: And I guess you're not. . . .

This exchange has succeeded in getting both partners frustrated and angry. Little has been resolved. Lisa and Tony would frequently sleep in separate rooms after an exchange like this. And yet, on closer examination, it was definitely possible to diffuse the communication at an early point; once the past was brought in, Lisa's angry feelings gained momentum. Tony was backed into a corner and there was little he could do or say to make things seem better to either of them.

This exchange can be diffused. Tony could have said, "You're right, Lisa, I'm terrible about being on time. Let's sit down together and see if we can think of ways to help me with this problem." Lisa could have said, "Okay, I accept your apology for now, but I really get angry about this and I want us to put our heads together and figure out what we can do to help you with this problem with tardiness." Either of those statements might have cut things off and helped avoid an escalation.

Say What You Want and What You Are Willing to Do

Always be clear about how you would like to see the problem or concern resolved, and be interested in what your partner wants as well. I believe it will always help if you state your willingness to work on a problem and your willingness to take the initiative. This way, your partner will always feel supported and have the experience of being half of a working partnership.

In the example of Tony and Lisa in the preceding section, I would suggest that Lisa make clear her willingness to help Tony figure out ways to be on time. Being late was more a problem for Lisa than it was for Tony, although tardiness had become more of an issue for Tony since he had married Lisa. If it were up to him alone, he would probably continue being late. His friends had adjusted to this reality and never expected him on time. Lisa had always been severely punished for being late, and was self-conscious about arriving anywhere late and causing disruptions. The couple had to face this problem and develop some ideas. Tony had to acknowledge that what was not a major concern to him affected Lisa, whom he loved. Lisa had to acknowledge that Tony's tardiness was not malicious but a habit he had built over a long period of time. The couple committed to working together on a mutual concern.

Listen to Your Partner and Reiterate What You Hear

To avoid misunderstandings, I suggest summarizing what you've heard your partner say. If the discussion gets lengthy, you can summarize not only what you've heard so far, but whatever decisions have been reached. It's possible to interrupt gently and ask, "Before you go any further, I just want to make sure I'm hearing you correctly. I heard you say . . . Is that correct so far?" Now your partner has an opportunity to correct any misunderstandings before you proceed. If specific fears surface during a conversation, don't let them build up. Stop your partner and let him or her know that something said has caused some confusion or pain. Before proceeding, make sure the communication is clarified.

Find Areas for Negotiation

Negotiating is an art. It requires partners in a relationship to give fifty-fifty. This ability to compromise can be foreign to survivors of childhood abuse because they grew up with their rights being violated and disregarded. It may take some time for survivors to believe and accept that their thoughts and feelings are important. It may also take some time for survivors to feel entitled to have their feelings taken into account.

In order for people to negotiate, each individual has to select areas for compromise. This is usually done by choosing the most critical issue, and acknowledging that some issues, while important, are not critical.

Kathy and Chuck had to negotiate for more time together. They discussed this problem and agreed that they were not happy with the amount of time they were spending together. Both of them had demanding jobs as well as specific activities they were not willing to give up. Kathy had aerobic and watercolor classes two evenings a week. She worked late two other evenings, and had a standing jogging date with a friend another evening. The weekend was committed to household chores such as gardening and washing clothes, and she stated that Sunday was a day set aside for resting and relaxing.

Chuck had a standing golf game on Sunday. He spent most of that day away. He worked late most evenings, and participated in some community organizations that required a portion of his evening time. In addition, since Kathy was not home on certain evenings, he stayed at work late, designing a special project on his own time. Chuck played cards with his neighbors twice a month, and watched a number of sports shows on TV.

The first thing this couple did was prioritize the essential and nonessential activities. Chuck chose the Sunday golf game and his card games as essential. Kathy chose aerobics and her evening work appointments as essential. It turned out that there were two evenings a week and one weekend day free, and the couple agreed to start with these times. This was a fairly easy negotiation because Chuck and Kathy agreed readily on what could be given up and what had to be retained.

If a couple cannot decide on what to give up and what to keep, it might be possible to use an external technique. Each person can write on a piece of paper those activities he or she is willing to give up; those activities not open for debate are not committed to paper. Each person also writes those activities he or she is not willing to give up, that is, the activities that will be retained. The papers are placed in a hat, and each person selects from each pile. The first chosen are either kept or given up. Each person keeps and gives up the same number of activities.

Agree to Disagree

Finally, there may come a time when partners must agree to disagree. There is nothing wrong with doing this, and it is frequently a good way to resolve a conflict.

Chuck and Kathy were always having heated arguments about politics. Both felt very strongly about their own views, and it was unlikely that either would feel swayed by the other's arguments. They finally realized that their arguments resulted in negative feelings, and they made a pact to simply agree to disagree. Each and every time they were about to get into one of these heated arguments, either Chuck or Kathy would say, "Oops, it's one of those times. Let's just agree to disagree." This became a symbolic way of putting down the swords and deciding not to fight. It worked very well for them and reduced the number of arguments significantly.

Practice

Remember that you are establishing patterns of interaction that you will use for the rest of your lives. You are building new habits and discarding old ones. This does not come easily. Practice is necessary. Set up situations where you can communicate about uncomplicated topics. As illustrated in an earlier example, you might want to set up nonthreatening subjects for communication. You might want to share your thoughts about a book you read, a movie you saw, a friend you have. Choose more and more intimate subjects as you go along. Remember that adult survivors of childhood abuse may need to build a tolerance for feelings of closeness and warmth. Thank your partner for sharing his or her thoughts.

Follow Up on Agreements

Make sure that you and your partner follow up on agreements made during your talks. Make a time to review how things have been going since the last time you talked and made agreements. Don't forget to check in and see how things are going, because if commitments are broken or forgotten, resentments can build and you may both end up feeling that talking does not produce results. The only way you'll feel motivated to talk more is if the talks have some positive results for both of you.

Chapter 7

FAMILY ROLES

The Spitting Image of . . .

I know I'm not fun to live with; I try really hard not to react to my husband as if he were a bad guy. But he just seems so much like my older brother, the one who used to beat me up. Every time my husband moves toward me quickly, or he tries to tickle me, I immediately get my guard up. I just wish I didn't think of them together.

Often people have asked me why it is that abused children are so loyal to their parents. They notice that abused children seem to love their parents, protect them, and want desperately to remain in their care. Why don't abused children reject their abusive parents? Why don't they become angry with them?

Not all abused children are the same; some abused children develop an antagonistic relationship with abusive parents or run away as soon as they are able to do so. But the angry or resentful feelings may emerge later. When young children are abused, they are caught in a double bind: their very existence depends on the people who hurt them. Because children urgently need physical affection and nurturing for their sur-

But he just seems so much like my older brother.

vival, they gravitate toward those people who care for them, expecting attention and affection. When parents or care-takers are abusive or neglectful, children assume that the reason for the abuse must be that they are unworthy of love, or that there is something inherently wrong with them. If you give young children a choice between who is bad—themselves or their parents—they will almost always choose themselves. They assume the responsibility in an effort to protect their parents; they idealize the parents, whom they need. At the same time, it may be that abused children believe that if they are bad, then their abuse is **something they can control;** by becoming good in their parents' eyes they can prevent their abuse.

Abused children who are deprived of necessary nurturing and guidance develop an intense longing for parental love. They wait patiently or make numerous attempts to alter their behavior in order to gain approval. This longing can persist into adulthood, and many adult survivors wait anxiously to receive the love they missed during formative years.

This becomes a great disadvantage to survivors since there is always an expectation that something or someone outside of themselves will eventually soothe and comfort them. They may enter intimate relationships expecting a quenching of deep-seated desires for caretaking. Some partners will feel overwhelmed by this expectation and may find themselves withdrawing out of fear or confusion.

Adult survivors have another grave disadvantage, which is that they did not have the example of a positive or safe intimate relationship. They were exposed to many unhealthy patterns of interaction, and they may feel uncertain about how to proceed in the face of an appropriate partner.

As I've mentioned elsewhere in this book, adult survivors have learned that relationships are loaded with inappropriate or unsafe interactions. Whether they were physically or sexually abused, neglected, or emotionally mistreated, the modeling of these inappropriate behaviors did occur and unfortunate lessons were learned. **What is familiar is comfortable; what is unfamiliar produces anxiety and fear.**

This precept is true for all of us. When we know what to expect, and what we expect happens, we are prepared and therefore less frightened by what we know. Let me illustrate this point by telling you about a woman I knew named Marta.

Marta was about twenty-five years old; she was attending a support group for adult survivors because she had been physically abused by her father, grandfather, and two older brothers. All men in her family were brutal and forced and coerced her into running their errands, cleaning the house, washing and ironing their clothes, doing their homework, and so on. She was now living with a man who treated her in pretty much the same way; when others asked her "how she put up with it," she didn't understand the question. The question presumed that she knew there was an alternative—she did not.

During the course of attending group therapy, Marta reported to members of the group that she was receiving positive attention from a man she worked with. From what she told the group, this man was easygoing and attentive. The other women in the group were excited for Marta and encouraged her to accept one of his many invitations to go out with him. Since the man Marta lived with, Paul, was at a weekly night out with the boys, she agreed to have dinner with the new beau.

She came to the next group meeting with a black eye. All of us gasped as she came in and we immediately asked her what had happened to her face. She gave the following account:

> I went to dinner. It was really nice, sort of. He asked me where I wanted to go eat. He asked me to decide what I wanted at the restaurant. He looked in my eyes a lot. He told me I looked really pretty. He asked me my opinions about lots of things. He actually seemed to want to hear what I thought and how I felt about stuff. I couldn't believe it. Once he reached over and

I got scared he was going to hit me, but he didn't. The whole thing made me really nervous, so I told him I was going to the bathroom and I left. When I got home, Paul knew I wasn't telling him the truth and he was really mad at me. I ended up telling him that I had gone out with this guy at work and he got really upset. You know, even though he got real jealous and he hit me some, at least with Paul I know where I stand.

As you can see in this example, Marta was so accustomed to being mistreated that when her new date was kind and attentive to her, she became extremely anxious. As she put it, "I couldn't stand the way he was being so nice to me, it made me so nervous that I had to get out of there." Her discomfort with him was parallel to her comfort with Paul's reaction when he learned that she had gone out with another guy. As Marta said so clearly, with Paul she knew exactly what to expect, which produced much less anxiety than trying to second-guess the other man's unfamiliar behavior.

What Marta would have to do to break the cycle of violence was to **tolerate** the unfamiliar behavior. She had to accept her anxiety and stay put even when she felt like leaving. She had to see for herself that nothing bad was going to happen. If she allowed others to treat her kindly, she would eventually begin to feel that she had a right to be treated well. And if her self-esteem increased, she would be less likely to tolerate abusive behavior from others. This is very hard work because the lessons of abuse are profound.

As survivors enter relationships with caring adults, a number of problems can surface, such as intense longing, expecting to be treated poorly, or feelings of anxiety or discomfort as partners are patient, understanding, kind, and committed. Partners will need to be cautious not to feel put off, frustrated, impatient, or retaliatory to survivor-partners who bring their childhood images of closeness with them.

Keep in mind the following:

- Take every opportunity to define who you are
- Talk about your own childhood lessons about relationships
- Talk to friends about relationships
- Surround yourself with people who can serve as role models
- Talk together, read, and practice
- Make your own traditions
- Start a scrapbook of your relationship
- Get an image of a positive relationship
- Give yourselves credit for interactions that you like
- Make a list of how you are like and unlike your parents
- Depersonalize but understand the connection
- Teach each other

Take Every Opportunity to Define Who You Are

This suggestion is consistent with many of the ideas mentioned before that have to do with open and ongoing communication. You must help your partner know you as fully as possible, making concerted efforts to talk about yourself. Tell your partner your preferences, your likes and dislikes; talk to him or her about your hopes for the future. Make yourself an open book. In this way your partner not only begins to know you better but can begin to see the differences between you and his or her parents or siblings. Remember that your partner has vast experience with the people from the past; experiences with you must be not only designed but documented. In other words, not only must you build a reservoir of memories between you, those memories must be acknowledged and recorded.

Talking about yourself may feel burdensome at first, particularly if you're unaccustomed to sharing yourself so fully. It's helpful if you consider it as "thinking out loud," and when you find yourself pondering something, take it as an opportunity to share with your partner, even if you think it's something uninteresting.

As you're watching TV or reading a book, you can talk to your partner about the situation you're observing and how you are reacting. Let your partner know what you agree or disagree with, what you would do in the position of the characters in the story, or what the story reminds you of.

One of the other advantages of this kind of communication is that you are able to demonstrate the sharing of inner thoughts and feelings. Even if your partner is bewildered about your random talking about yourself, the end result may be that he or she not only becomes comfortable with talking but will reciprocate with some spontaneous comments of his or her own.

Talk About Your Own Childhood Lessons About Relationships

To counter the negative or frightening experiences of your partner's childhood, share your own experiences. Your partner may feel incredulous but interested as well. In my experience, adult survivors are engrossed by information about "normal" lives and how other people behave in families. They may ask questions and may find some of the material very hard to understand. At the same time, this new information serves as a kind of comparison base, so that your partner can see firsthand that there are alternatives to abusive patterns set by parents or caretakers.

You might even add to your own knowledge base by contacting some of your extended family members and asking them to write you letters about their memories of your childhood. Often, isolated family members find it appealing to be asked to contribute in this way. Those letters can be read to your partner and may give him or her another way of understanding other perspectives on family life.

If you also had an abusive background, you probably need to let each other know as much as you can about your backgrounds, and the impact your experiences have had on your lives. You also need to acknowledge that both of you enter a relationship with a clear disadvantage: You do not have the positive experiences to draw from. Your efforts need to be directed toward developing a foundation on which to build the positive interactions in your relationship. Be careful to avoid situations where you constantly compare how bad your backgrounds were. I've seen partners get into a kind of competition about whose experience was better or worse. This doesn't serve a good purpose and keeps you focused on the past in a negative way. Remember that the past cannot be relived and that you have the power to shape your future into a new and rewarding one.

Talk to Friends About Relationships

Another way to equip yourself with healthy perspectives will be to select friends you feel comfortable with and engage them in conversations about their relationships. People usually like to talk about themselves, and you may find it easy to get people talking. Here are some questions you might ask when you are conversing naturally. Avoid asking too many questions in a row because some people might feel self-conscious about answering too many questions.

What kinds of things do you do to have fun?
How do you make sure you have enough time to spend
   together as a couple?
How do you get along with your parents now?
How do you usually celebrate birthdays or holidays?
   What happens when each of you has a different way?

What happens when you get angry with each other? How do you usually let each other know you're angry?

How do you usually solve disagreements?

Does your partner ever remind you of your parents? Is that good or bad?

Do you have things you like to do together and things you like to do apart?

What's the best part of your relationship? What's the worst?

What do you like best about your partner?

What do you like least about your partner?

Has your partner changed a lot since you started living together or got married?

How do you work out disagreements?

What's the most romantic thing you do together?

How do you keep romance alive?

Now obviously, some of these questions are more personal than others, and you will have to decide which questions to ask depending on how close you are to specific friends. As I said earlier, don't ask these questions in a row because it can feel like an interrogation, but wait for times in the conversation when there is an opportunity and one of these questions might be asked. Your friends may not want to answer and that's okay, but many couples enjoy having these conversations and they can be a way of getting closer. Along the same line, when you find yourself in a situation in which you see few options, ask your friends what they do. For example, if you get depressed and can't figure out a way to feel better, ask friends what they do. You may be surprised to find that everyone has had this experience at one time or another and has developed unique solutions that you can then try yourself.

This might be a difficult thing to do. Survivors usually feel

Surround yourself with people who can serve as role models.

more comfortable with other survivors, and that is perfectly all right. It is also helpful to attempt friendships with people of different backgrounds as well. This is especially true if survivors have friends in various degrees of recovery, or who are currently involved in unsafe or destructive relationships of their own. In these cases, a survivor needs to be as supportive as possible, making sure that friends' problems don't get assumed. In addition, I encourage survivors to work on forming and establishing relationships with others who might give them added insights into, and healthy models of, how intimate relationships work.

If you have friends or work acquaintances who would provide this opportunity, try to arrange informal activities for you and your partner. Plan activities that don't put too much pressure on either of you; it may be particularly difficult for him or her to meet new people and develop confidence about interacting with others. You might want to meet your new friends at a theater and watch a movie together. Watching a film requires little conversation and can be enjoyable to all. If you make a dinner date, rather than have friends come to your house, have your friends meet you at a restaurant and drive separately. If your partner feels uncomfortable, you are poised to make a quick exit; you can stay longer if you both feel comfortable.

Talk Together, Read, and Practice

There is nothing wrong with wanting to enhance your relationship. As a matter of fact, wanting to strengthen your relationship is commendable.

This is a wonderful time to strive for self-improvement because there is so much material available for people who want to pursue learning about important topics such as communication skills, building trust, fighting fair, and so on. All couples struggle with similar fears, worries, and concerns. The only difference is that some individuals enter an intimate partnership with the strong foundation of knowing about the nature of healthy relationships and how to relate in a loving and respectful way. Be sure you don't feel judgmental toward yourself or your partner if you seem to have ongoing difficulties. Each difficulty can present you with a new challenge and a new lesson. Each time a conflict is faced and resolved, you and your partner are building an arsenal of useful experiences.

Make Your Own Traditions

Survivors of childhood abuse either have sparse memories about positive rituals or traditions in their families of origin, or the rituals they remember may be ones that are scary, hurtful, or negative. For example, a traditionally happy holiday such as Thanksgiving may bring up memories in your partner of fighting, alcoholic outbursts, or sexual abuse.

Survivors will need your help to feel comfortable with the concept of designing their own traditions. Too often survivors feel stigmatized by or ashamed of their unhappy childhoods and may believe they have little to contribute to forming traditions in their new relationships.

As a partner of a survivor, you can help by bringing this subject up when it is relevant. As holidays or potential celebrations get close, talk to your partner about how the two of you would like to commemorate the occasion. You can offer some suggestions not only from your own family but perhaps by drawing on the experiences of friends or colleagues. Decide together what you choose to do as a couple and at some point or another after the celebration occurs, take an opportunity to talk about how you liked the event and the aspects you wish to repeat in the future.

In order to remind yourself and your partner of the memories you are creating together, get a scrapbook and fill it in on a regular basis. You can use mementos of special occasions along with photographs of your happy times together. Take the scrapbook out and look at it often, validating the positive feelings symbolized in the scrapbook.

Scrapbooks will be varied in content. One couple I knew had photos of the first time they did anything new together. Included were pictures of first holiday celebrations, first Valentine's Day, birthdays, anniversaries, and the like. Both partners rejoiced in showing the scrapbook to friends and extended family; it was prominently displayed in the living

Start a scrapbook of your relationship.

room. Each time they looked at the pictures they felt close to each other and became future-oriented. Many adult survivors have difficulty with planning ahead or visualizing their future. Having had abusive and traumatic experiences in childhood creates feelings of vulnerability and futility in adult survivors; planning ahead, therefore, may be a foreign concept.

Get an Image of a Positive Relationship

It can be difficult to find couples to emulate. You may not know too many couples, or you may not socialize with couples or people who are in a relationship. If this is the case for you and your partner, you need to look to other places for models to emulate.

Many individuals like to watch television. If this is a preference of yours, attempt to select shows in which couples demonstrate a positive regard within an intimate relationship or friendship. Try to pay attention to the qualities that are admired. In other words, try to explain to yourself and your partner what it is about the couple on TV that strikes your fancy. Be specific. Stay away from vague comments such as "They seem to get along together," and try to explain why you are under that impression. What do they say or do that makes you perceive them as a couple that gets along?

Once you've studied the couple and understand why you seem impressed with them, share that with your partner and ask what he or she thinks. Move on to asking if your partner has an admired couple on TV. Have a conversation together about the qualities most revered in relationships. You will learn a great deal from your partner by discussing TV preferences.

Likewise you may have a favorite film or book in which a relationship exemplifies qualities you would like to emulate. Finally, if no ideal couple is found, use your imagination and create fantasy characters and make them behave and communicate in ways you believe are valuable. Create situations for your fantasy couple and watch what they do and say. By imagining desired behaviors, you can gain inspiration and motivation to behave in more positive and rewarding ways.

Give Yourselves Credit for Interactions That You Like

Survivors of childhood abuse have difficulty giving or receiving compliments. It's not that they don't feel grateful, appreciative, or loving; it's that they often can't find the words to express what they feel and may lack the means to show adequately their inner feelings. Survivors may also feel uncomfortable with positive attention and may appear embarrassed or uncomfortable when praised.

Make your comments brief and precise. As I've said previously, describe what you're talking about. "You were so organized" is less clear than "I am impressed with how organized you are when you write down the chores you have to do and then put a line through them as you complete them."

Make a List of How You Are Like and Unlike Your Parents

This is a useful and informative exercise for both you and your partner. Adult survivors may have a tendency to perceive people or situations from a vulnerable position. In other words, they may expect that a partner will disapprove of them because disapproval has been a consistent past response. Survivors may even be drawn to people who have qualities similar to those of their abusive families. This is not because they are masochistic; survivors don't want to be hit or hurt. Survivors are drawn to those behaviors that are either consciously or unconsciously familiar. I've been mentioning this dynamic throughout the book, and survivors need all the help they can get to distinguish between abusive family members and their current friends and lovers.

Begin by suggesting the idea for yourself. Tell your partner that you have been pondering the similarities and differences between yourself and your parents and/or siblings. Generate a written list that you then share with your partner, asking for his or her perceptions on the subject.

Next, encourage your partner to develop a similar list. Help by adding your general impressions. Take care to be as objective as possible; survivors may feel protective of their parents, and while they may feel comfortable making their own judgments, they may resent or ignore yours.

After this exercise is completed, and particularly if the communication has gone well, enter into a discussion of how your partner is like and unlike your own parents. In other words, you have first each made comparisons between yourselves and your parents. Now compare yourselves to your in-laws. This way you broach the subject of how your partner is similar or dissimilar to your parents or siblings.

Depersonalize but Understand the Connection

When your survivor-partner reacts to you as if you were the hurtful or abusive or neglecting parent from his or her past, make every effort both to understand why this is happening, and to view it as a natural response that has little to do with you, and much more to do with the fact that past experiences do create current vulnerabilities. These vulnerabilities make your partner susceptible to conditioned responses that take time to change. It can be important to remind yourself that changes will occur for your partner, and you can contribute by being safe and consistent. It is only through consistent and predictable safe care over time that your partner will develop a tolerance for (and trust of) positive and kind interactions. You cannot make your partner trust you; you can, however, show you are trustworthy.

Teach Each Other

Finally, there is an inherent benefit in being half of a friendship or intimate relationship: There are two people to work together and learn from each other.

Many individuals are underprepared to establish or maintain intimate relationships whether or not they were abused or neglected. Even individuals who were raised in "functional" families can have chronic or situational difficulties as they grapple with the challenge of establishing relationships.

You and your partner can definitely learn to trust each other, learn about each other's backgrounds, differentiate between what your childhood was like and what you want for your future, and you can acknowledge the positive outcomes of nurturing your intimacy. At the same time, you can recognize the things you don't know and are willing to learn from each other.

Feel confident about opening up to your partner. Know that honesty will contribute to ongoing trust and communication. Share your fears as well as your aspirations, and try to balance the subjects you discuss. If you find you spend too much time pondering the unhappy events in your life, try to generate conversation about happier topics. Remember that each day you are creating a new history and background together, and this background will serve you well in the future.

Chapter 8

COMMITMENT

I don't know why, but every time something comes up about the future, even something dumb like how we'll celebrate our anniversary next year, she gets really upset and cries, and I just don't get it. The next thing I know, she'll be upset or angry because she's afraid I'm going to leave her.

Adults abused as children grew up with parents or caretakers who did little to inspire hope about the future. Nonabused children may have parents who encourage them to think five or ten years into the future, and imagine what they might like to be doing. Nonabused children also have numerous experiences that are rewarding, therefore reinforcing, and these experiences create both an expectation that good things will happen in their lives, and a desire to re-create the happy or exciting feelings.

The opposite can be said about children growing up in abusive and unrewarding families; little direction or inspiration about the pleasures that can be derived from living is provided. Abusive parents for the most part are individuals who are not happy, excited, and feeling in control of their own destinies. They cannot model a full range of feelings because they frequently come from emotionally empty families themselves. It is sad to think that unhealthy and unhappy patterns and expectations can be passed down from generation to generation, but it's encouraging to know that giving these patterns care and attention can result in breaking the cycle of abuse.

Abused children have many disappointments, frustrations, and negative experiences. They learn to expect little. They are emotionally understimulated, and it would be just as unreasonable for us to expect that these children develop into happy adults without some outside help, as it would be to expect that a plant would thrive and grow healthy and strong without proper environmental conditions.

If your partner was abused as a child, he or she may have experienced not only the emotional emptiness I described above, but, in addition, there may have been a number of inherent threats that caused him or her to think about survival on a "one day at a time" basis. An abused child does not have the reserve psychic energy to imagine the future as different; all energies are directed toward surviving daily threats. Drawing on an analogy I gave earlier about walking through a field with hidden swamps, an abused child must concentrate on maneuvering through the threatening environment. Planning for the future will not be a priority for an endangered child until the immediate threat is removed.

If your partner was abused as a child, he or she must concentrate on maneuvering through whatever current threats are perceived or exist. His or her whole existence focuses on staying safe at all cost. And even though you may do your very best to create a safe and loving situation, as we have seen earlier, your partner's perception of danger stems more from internal experiences than from anything that you say or do directly. The situation itself—being in an intimate relationship or close friendship—may feel like a boxer's ring where two people are likely to engage in deadly combat.

Until your partner understands intellectually and senses emotionally that the situation is safe, his or her guard must be in place. Anticipation and preparation were valued survival skills.

One other factor comes into play when discussing the topic of commitment: It should be kept in mind that most abused children have faced countless disappointments in their lives. They have hoped for change and longed for their needs to be met. Few changes have occurred in the past, and their needs have gone unrecognized and unmet. A valuable protective strategy is to give up expecting anything. If you expect nothing, you are spared intense disappointment. Unfortunately, a child who gives up hope never has a chance to find out about life's rewarding situations.

One adult survivor confided to me that as soon as she fell in love with someone, she felt the need to withdraw from the relationship. Her need to run away was easy to understand: Leave them before you care too much; if you care, they'll leave you or hurt you some other way. In this case, the woman's alarm signal was her sense of caring or being cared for. Once the alarm rang, her response was swift and decisive. This response had obviously been useful to her when she was a child and couldn't depend on her drug-addicted parents. However, as an adult, it was unfortunate that she had not been able to experiment with recognizing the clue, tolerating the intense fear, and deciding to explore the safety or lack of safety of a new situation. While she stayed safe from anticipated abandonment and pain, she also kept herself shielded from potentially loving and rewarding exchanges. It was only when she was able to tolerate the anxiety and master her fear sufficiently enough to wait the alarm signal out and explore further, that she was able to establish intimacy and learn about the parameters of a loving and positive exchange. It is not easy to tolerate anxiety, however, and doing so requires a great deal of courage. This survivor developed the ability to choose what to do with her fear and nervousness, and she learned how to scout around further to determine if the threat was real and current.

If you have encountered difficulties with your partner about commitments, remember that this is a troublesome area. As a nurturing parent or caretaker might do with a child, you can help by removing any pressure about decision making and by focusing instead on modeling behaviors that encourage the setting of goals and the laying out of plans to meet those goals.

Consider doing the following:

- Talk about yourself as a child
- Talk about tasks you have undertaken
- Talk about individual goals in your work
- Talk about individual goals that are concrete
- Talk about individual goals that are abstract
- Set small goals for your relationship

Talk About Yourself as a Child

Broach this subject by giving some examples of accomplishments in your childhood that required your commitment to something or someone while keeping an eye on an end goal.

Simon gave his wife Linda the following example:

When I was nine I wanted a bike really bad, but at the same time I was afraid to get on one because I didn't know how to ride one. My dad said that he wouldn't spend money on a bike until he was sure I could ride one and I would like it, and until I earned ten dollars on my own. It took me a year to get that bike! I earned ten cents for each yard I could rake up the leaves, and so it took me one hundred yards to earn the money. Sometimes I felt it wasn't worth the effort because even if I got the money, my dad wanted me to know how to ride first. Once I got the money, though, I talked to my best friend, Steve, and asked him if he could show me how to ride the bike in his garage where no one could see me and laugh. Steve was the only person in the world I felt totally comfortable with probably because no matter what I was afraid of, he always told me it was okay and that he had felt that way before also. Steve taught me, and one year later I got my bike. My mom threw in a horn and painted wheels because she knew how hard I had worked.

After relating this story, Simon spontaneously revealed that he had learned a great lesson about commitment from setting a goal, developing clear steps toward the goal, and then persevering. He told his wife this was the first time he had seen that he had the power to make things happen, and that he could be patient as long as there was a plan and he knew he was working on this plan. Linda was surprised by this revelation since she had had no experiences that had shown her she could work for something and succeed. Simon was quick to point out that Linda had gotten very good grades in school and that she must have put some planning into homework to obtain the high marks. Linda remarked, "That was easy; Mom was usually drunk and passed out on the couch, or she was 'out.' There was nothing for me to do but study, and when I went to school, the teacher seemed to think that I was pretty smart." Linda was getting some of her needs for nurturing and approval met through her teacher, and she had learned to focus her energies academically in an effort to feel less lonely and confused.

The story that Simon told Linda, and his gentle reminder that she had made exceptional academic accomplishments, quietly encouraged Linda to pursue some educational interests in her adult life. She commented that as she approached this education a little voice inside her said, "Why are you wasting your time?" and "You'll amount to nothing." I asked her to create a new inner voice that said, "You are smart and you deserve a chance to pursue your interests." I encouraged her to affirm her choices frequently and loudly. She told me that after a while the negative voice ("which is really annoying because it sounds just like my mother") was heard only sporadically. Her own new voice had become "sturdy and confident." Linda did very well in school, and at first Simon's interest in her school progress was unfamiliar, therefore bothersome. Eventually Linda was able to show Simon her work and seemed to delight in his obvious pride in her accomplishments. Linda was now getting her needs met directly from her partner rather than turning to the teacher to get her needs met. Her self-esteem increased, and her sense of being in a safe and rewarding partnership was enhanced.

Talk About Tasks You Have Undertaken

This is a similar way of introducing the subject of commitment, but it draws from adult experiences rather than childhood. One potential drawback of relating childhood experiences is that your partner may feel more stigmatized or "different" because of differences in your childhood experiences. The comparison may, in fact, elicit feelings of deprivation and longing, or generate a sense of how unfair the world has been.

You might want to select a story to relate that draws from adulthood, when parental figures were no longer in the picture. You might want to talk about how you decided about a career and then chose the areas of study that would best prepare you in that direction. You might want to talk about a time you made a decision to pursue something and how you went about doing that.

Talk About Individual Goals in Your Work

If you are currently employed, you might want to illustrate the concept of commitment and how it is used in a variety of settings by discussing specific projects that you work on and how you set long-term goals, or by using examples from your colleagues. Interestingly enough, many of the organizational frameworks for setting and obtaining goals presume a commitment to the project and a willingness to follow through on plans designed to move the project toward completion. During the implementation phase, different points are set up to evaluate ongoing progress and make adjustments. These basic principles are definitely useful in intimate relationships. They encourage a definition of goals, a time frame for completion, steps to be taken, and opportunities for review and adjustment.

Talk About Individual Goals That Are Concrete

Another area you might talk about with your partner is how you go about making a commitment to projects around the house. In this area, point to a problem that needed fixing and describe how you made the decision to tackle the problem and how you proceeded. Even though this sounds very basic, it is exactly this kind of clear illustration that can help your partner get a sense of commitment and planning for the future. Most children are encouraged in these ways by parents, caretakers, or teachers who help them set ends and devise the means for completion.

Talk about how you went about fixing an oven, a television, or a household appliance. A friend of mine recently took a year to design a fruit garden in his backyard. He first made the decision to plant, discussed the types of fruits he, his wife, and his children most wanted, and then laid out where the trees would go given the space in the backyard. He then got the trees and planted them one by one, revising his plan as needed. The trees will be yielding fruit in another year and the garden is a source of pride for every member of the family.

By discussing commitments in your childhood, your young adulthood, your work, or regarding household chores, you are describing a wide range of experiences with commitment. These will probably be much less threatening to someone frightened by planning ahead, and once you have talked about these subjects in passing, you might move to the use of commitment for personal goals.

Talk About Individual Goals That Are Abstract

When you approach this area, it is important that you talk about yourself in a retrospective way. You might just start by saying, "You know, I was thinking how I've changed what I do in the morning." Now you've probably got your partner's attention. "I remember about ten years ago I would always wake up late. I was always grumpy because I felt rushed, I would get to work in a bad mood, and I always felt grouchy because I didn't get a chance to eat. I talked to some friends of mine who told me how they got up and used the early morning time to read, listen to music, eat a good breakfast, and then they would go to work. At first I thought it was crazy, but then I decided since my way wasn't working, I would try their way. Boy, was that hard at first. But I kept at it until I actually began to enjoy my morning time, and now that we're together, I especially enjoy sitting with you in the morning and touching base before we both run off."

This communication is about commitment to make a change for very personal reasons. The goals were to feel better and more relaxed and centered before dashing off to work. There were behavioral ways to accomplish those goals, but the goals were personal and more abstract as compared with a garden that's planted, an item that's repaired, and so on.

Set Small Goals for Your Relationship

Proceed with care when you approach the topic of commitment regarding your relationship. Don't push or pressure your partner. Try to talk about things you may want for yourself. You might want to say things about the future that are nonthreatening, such as "When that movie comes out, let's go see it" or "When Willie Nelson is in town, let's make a date to go listen to him." You can also participate in things that require small commitments, like joining a bowling league or softball team, or planning to attend something you like such as the baseball or football games in your area. As you make these commitments make sure you validate the process. "Remember we talked about going to see Willie Nelson four months ago; he's in town and I can get tickets today." Your partner needs to build a background of positive incidents related to making and keeping commitments.

The next area to approach is that of the personal relationship. First, choose less alarming areas. Don't start with something you know may create anxiety; determine a safe topic and set a time frame **for yourself.** Simply "wonder out loud" about your partner's participation. An example might be "I'm going to give myself another three months on this job. Then I'm going to sit down and review what I like and don't like, and make a decision about asking for a transfer or thinking about a new job. I'm sure there are some things that are fine about the job and some things that aren't. Maybe you can be thinking to yourself what I may have mentioned to you in the past, so in three months we can talk about it together." You are talking about a commitment that you've made to addressing an area of concern for yourself. At the same time, you are asking your partner to participate in your process by suggesting that he or she may want to be thinking about this and may be available for discussion down the line. You are not making a demand and you are not pressuring, but you are taking the time to set a time frame, and then follow through. You are allowing and inviting your partner to be part of your process of making a commitment and following through.

Chapter 9

RELAXING AND REDUCING STRESS

*I feel he's tight as a drum. He never lets his guard down.
He's thinking all the time, working all the time, reading
business magazines. I just wish he could slow down sometimes. I worry that he's digging an early grave for himself.*

Abused children have usually felt unsafe in their own skins.
The concept of the body being safe is foreign, as is the idea
that the body could produce pleasurable sensations. Abused
children are usually frightened and vigilant. They live in
inconsistent, unrewarding, and explosive environments that
produce tension and anxiety. Consequently, abused children
hold in their feelings, afraid to recognize or express themselves. The body becomes a container that must be kept
tightly sealed. As negative or uncomfortable feelings are
withheld, positive or warm feelings are also disregarded. The
abused child protects himself from difficult feelings and at
the same time positive feelings are compromised.

In addition to feeling unsafe in his or her body, the abused
child has little understanding about feelings in general. Abusive parents may have stifled all expression of feelings in their

children, or may have modeled inappropriate and extreme ways of showing their feelings. In the latter case, children shy away from showing their feelings, since this display is associated with feelings of terror, pain, or sorrow.

If your partner was abused as a child, you may have noticed that he or she flinches or startles easily, or, conversely, may act oblivious to events or situations that feel surprising or frightening to you. In either case, your partner has to cope with his or her lack of familiarity with physical and emotional comfort and relaxation.

You can't "talk" someone out of feelings of tension or fear. When your partner perceives less threat, he or she will have less physical and emotional tension. At the same time, you can't "walk on eggshells," hesitant to speak or behave naturally for fear of upsetting or triggering your partner. If you do this, you will slowly be training yourself to become tense and uncomfortable.

One of the ways to be helpful, without being demanding or placing expectations on your partner, is to do what parents have done for centuries with their children: model the appropriate behavior without making demands. We all learn from watching the important people in our lives.

Jeff and Darla had very different backgrounds. Jeff had a fairly happy childhood, with strong positive relationships with both his parents. He had experienced some stressful times, including the death of his mother when he was twelve, but he had always had a supportive, kind, and warm family who gave him a great deal of attention and always made him feel special.

Darla came from a dysfunctional family in which she always felt invisible. They spent very little time together as a family, and Darla felt isolated and lonely. Her father was an alcoholic who made a disruption every night when he came home; a loud and vicious fight between mother and father usually followed his arrival. Darla witnessed numerous beatings between her parents. Her mother was physically violent to her father when he was so inebriated that he could not defend himself physically; her father was physically abusive of her mother and Darla's older sister at other times. Darla was never physically abused by her father or mother, yet she was always worried that she would eventually be targeted by them. Darla was physically abused by her older sister, Terry, who was resentful and angry with her younger sister. Terry had been delegated the role of caretaker to Darla and her younger brother, and consequently she did not experience a happy childhood or adolescence. Terry was a harsh and demanding caretaker, often threatening to hurt her younger siblings and locking them in closets when they misbehaved. Jeff insisted that he and Darla see a counselor, primarily because he felt frustrated at Darla's discomfort. He described their relationship as good, and he clearly loved his wife. Darla seemed devoted to her husband and spoke quietly about all the aspects of the relationship she liked.

As Jeff described the problem in the relationship, he said he was concerned that Darla was always tense and afraid. He hated that she seemed afraid of him when he raised his voice, or when he reached over suddenly. Jeff wanted Darla to relax and to feel confident about him. He stated that he would never hit Darla and he would never leave her, and he wanted her to stop worrying about doing or saying things that were wrong, or, as she would say, "would get her into trouble."

I made the following suggestions to this couple:

- Discuss ways of relaxing
- Increase pleasurable experiences
- Visualize relaxed states
- Practice and enhance relaxation skills
- Make time commitments to relaxation
- Exercise
- Learn to play

Discuss Ways of Relaxing

Your partner is probably unfamiliar with the concept of relaxing, so you must take the lead by talking about ways of relaxing that you have found effective. Think back to specific strategies for bringing your stress level down; give your partner the details of how they work and how they are useful. If you are equally unfamiliar with ways to relax, ask friends or family about their practices, or go to your local bookstore or library and read some books on the topic. Too much stress is one of the ills of the century, and countless books on the subject have been written.

As with other suggestions I have made, be sure that you begin by discussing only yourself. If you can, demonstrate your willingness to learn about relaxing by making the time to practice positive habits regarding repose. Be sure you communicate what you are doing and how it feels to you. Your partner's interest in relaxation may be piqued by watching you. He or she may ask questions or simply watch with interest.

Increase Pleasurable Experiences

Adult survivors tend to feel uncomfortable and unsafe inside their skins. Their bodies have not yielded pleasurable sensations; instead, their bodies have withstood rejections, intrusions, and pain.

Try to think about physical comfort and pleasure. Remind yourself of activities or experiences that felt satisfying and joyful; share those with your partner.

Try to initiate a range of activities that might bring you and your partner pleasant sensations. Think about activities that are safe, nonthreatening, and fun. For example, swimming, walking in the forest, lying in the sun, a picnic on the grass, eating cold fruit on a summer day, making sand castles,

. . . making a sand castle

walking through a museum, playing catch, making bread, running, or playing a sport are ways of experiencing pleasant, warm sensations. If your partner is reluctant, see if he or she can tell you more about the hesitations. For example, one woman I knew wanted very much to swim, but was afraid to be inside a closed environment when doing so. To her delight, her partner located an outdoor pool nearby. Another woman was afraid to go walking through a forest alone, but found great comfort in walking her new dog through the peaceful environment.

Visualize Relaxed States

Visualization has been used to accomplish a number of positive goals. The healing professions have long recognized the effectiveness of having patients visualize the healing process.

Cancer victims have been counseled to imagine their healthy cells multiplying and becoming strong enough to successfully battle the unhealthy cells. Athletes use visualization during their training programs to help in the setting and meeting of goals. The philosophy is that if you can imagine (visualize) yourself doing something, you will have a greater likelihood not only of making the effort, but of succeeding.

Visualization provides someone with the opportunity for a safe rehearsal of an unfamiliar or feared activity or interaction. Your partner may not be able to relax or engage in a pleasant experience at the outset, but he or she may be able to imagine doing so.

Let your partner know about visualization by giving an example of how you have tried or used a visualization technique. Encourage him or her to experiment with you. Your partner can select an activity or situation that would be relaxing to him or her and then develop a fantasy in which the event occurs and the outcome is safe and surprisingly pleasant.

Practice and Enhance Relaxation Skills

None of us relaxes easily in this busy and stressful world; few of us have been taught how to relax. Luckily, there is currently a great deal of information available on how to reduce stress and relax. Physicians are agreed that managing stress is one of the most relevant preventive health measures to be taken.

There is little that is magical or mystical about relaxing. Relaxation occurs when the body undergoes certain physiological changes.

To relax, the body must be allowed to rest in a comfortable position. Oxygen must be inhaled and exhaled rhythmically and comfortably. The body's muscles must be systematically relaxed. For example, the fists can be tightened and then relaxed; the forehead can be furrowed and then relaxed. You can do this from head to toe until you have focused on each part of the entire body in an attempt to get the circulation moving and the body experiencing comfortable and warm sensations. Preferences vary about how to achieve deep relaxation; some people listen to relaxation tapes, while others listen to classical music.

As with anything else, it is important to practice relaxing; there are initial feelings of awkwardness. Eventually, relaxing becomes desirable and habitual.

Make Time Commitments to Relaxation

Obviously, new habits require attention and effort. Decide when you can make the time to relax, and whether you do it alone or with your partner, make sure you follow through so you are building habits over time.

Exercise

Most physicians recommend that individuals exercise in a comfortable way. They suggest that diet and exercise prevent many chronic and acute medical emergencies.

Adult survivors have probably been reticent to engage in physical movement; they will need to find their own rate and frequency of activity. They may feel hesitant to exercise in public or to participate in competitive sports. They will need to find unique and comfortable ways of gently introducing their bodies to the pleasure of safe and free movement.

Learn to Play

Finally, most adult survivors did not learn how to play in childhood. They were unable to employ play fully as a way to express their feelings and communicate. They may feel disinclined to do so now, and yet it can be remarkably helpful to adult survivors to learn how to play.

You may have some playful activities that you enjoy. Perhaps there will be one or two that your partner can be encouraged to try. Try some basic play activities like throwing and catching balls, playing cards, or running through sprinklers. You might want to talk to friends and get more ideas. Keep presenting the options, modeling your own sense of joy, and taking opportunities to fill your lives with pleasurable experiences.

Chapter 10

THERAPY

The Solution or the Problem?

I want her to go see a therapist badly. But the subject is taboo. I'm not allowed to bring it up. She sees therapy as a sign of mental illness; she thinks when I suggest she see someone, that I'm telling her she's crazy. She also says she can't possibly talk to a stranger, and that no one will understand her. How can I get her to see that she needs to go?

Therapy can be a frightening proposition to anyone; to adult survivors it can seem terrifying.

Therapy is a one-to-one relationship where the focus is on the client or patient. The therapist is an authority figure who asks personal questions and waits to hear the patient's inner thoughts and feelings. There is an assumption that the therapist can "see through" the patient's defenses, and will make interpretations about the information the patient shares.

Survivors usually feel uncomfortable about being visible or audible. Their defense strategies have included keeping a low profile; they may even believe that no one will ever be truly interested in them or consider them important enough to listen. At the same time, their experiences with authority figures have been negative; their assumptions are that they will be punished or hurt. They have not been encouraged to be introspective, may lack a language to communicate their thoughts and feelings, and may not have methods to cope with anxiety or fear. The idea of making the first phone call may be overwhelming, and attempts to do so may have caused great anticipatory fear and discomfort. Many adult

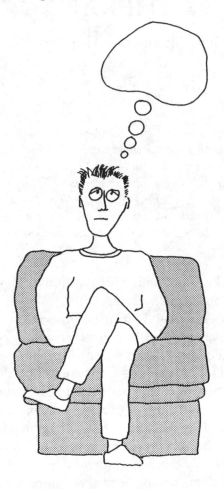

Needless to say, many adult survivors have amnesia.

survivors were either overtly threatened with harm to keep quiet, or they sensed the danger in speaking to others about private matters. Survivors may also develop fierce loyalty to their abusive parents, guarding the secrets of the family; or they may idealize their parents, taking on the responsibility for the abuse. All of these feelings will interfere with survivors' ability to disclose the facts as they are remembered. Needless to say, many adult survivors have amnesia regarding the events of their childhood, and may feel uncomfortable about entering therapy without clear memories.

It also goes without saying that the stigma of psychotherapy persists in some communities; it is much more acceptable to be in therapy now than ever before, but this acceptance is subject to cultural and regional differences.

The availability of services for adult survivors also differs among communities, yet the issue of childhood abuse has become so well recognized that it is rare to find a community without some available services. Several national hotlines have been set up to provide referral information to survivors of childhood abuse. (See referrals at the end of the book.)

If it appears to you that your partner may benefit from therapy, remember that you can make a suggestion but it will be your partner's decision whether or not to seek therapy. You are best advised to bring the subject up from time to time, without pressuring or nagging. Your partner needs to hear that you believe therapy will be helpful and that it is available to individuals with a range of problems. You might explain that you regard the need for therapy not as a sign of weakness but rather as a sign of strength. The reality is that it takes great courage and determination to explore painful subjects.

Let your partner know that the area of childhood abuse and its impact has been well studied in the last fifteen years or so, and that there are many known problem areas that can develop as a result of abuse. You can let your partner know that most survivors struggle with feelings of fear of new people and situations, difficulty trusting others, and persistent feelings of being unworthy or undeserving of love. These are normal feelings, given the way they were raised; these are also feelings that can change with a little help in understanding their origins.

Survivors of childhood abuse must confront their pasts so that they can focus on the present and the future. The goal of therapy is to help the individual get unstuck from the past. To do this, there must be an initial exploration of past events.

Some survivors fear that going into therapy will do the opposite: that it will keep them "dwelling" on things that cannot be changed. Most therapists want to listen and understand the past events, but will more often than not try to make the connections between the past and present difficulties, and will focus on helping the client with here-and-now problems. The only way to disengage from the past is to face it, process the feelings, and get some closure so there can be forward movement.

It might be helpful for your partner to read some books written by survivors about their recovery process—there are many. It might also be helpful for your partner to talk to someone at a hot line about therapy and what it entails. Taking these steps will usually lower some of the fears or concerns about going to therapy.

But your partner is not the only one in need of support and assistance. You are entitled to some help as well. We have been talking about many of the feelings of partners of adult survivors. Even though you can say to yourself, "He or she is the one who really needs help," remember that you are in a unique situation. You are the "other half" of an intimate relationship in which there are some difficulties. You are entitled to feel impatient, worried, angry, frustrated, or helpless. The person you love suffers within the relationship, and you may feel that you are the cause of the suffering. You want to be helpful and yet may not know how. You want to be supportive and yet may find that your support is met with rejection. You may become annoyed that you are bearing the brunt of something someone else did; you may want to kill the person who hurt your partner, and yet that person may be your partner's parent or sibling. You may even have to maintain a civil relationship with that parent because your partner insists that the abuse cannot be openly discussed.

You may end up feeling guilty for your lack of patience, or your frustration. You may feel impatient that the therapy is taking so long, or making things worse, or not helping at all. You can harbor fantasies of leaving your partner, and yet hate yourself for your insensitivity.

You can also benefit from therapy, and a valuable resource that has surfaced in the recent past is support groups for partners of survivors. You will be pleasantly surprised to find that you are not alone! You will also be amazed at how much you have in common with other people who live with and love adult survivors. But most importantly, you will have an opportunity to acknowledge your own feelings, your own pain and suffering, and hear some suggestions about how to help yourself and remain available to your partner as well.

Even if you believe that you are not the one who was abused and therefore not the one who needs help, remember that your ultimate goal is to be supportive of your partner through his or her recovery process, and you may need some help to be of further assistance.

Here are some common concerns that have been raised by partners or friends of adult survivors regarding the issue of therapy.

They Won't Hear of It

As mentioned above, therapy is a very individual decision and your partner may need to think about therapy for a long while before making the decision and following through. Try to provide some basic information in a matter-of-fact way; you might read some books about recovery from abuse and then leave them around the house for your partner to read. You might provide phone numbers for therapists or hot lines. Be sure you are conveying your acceptance of therapy as helpful and appropriate to individuals who have been hurt as children. Don't be pushy, but be sure that you don't drop the subject completely.

It Makes Them Worse

Another concern occurs when the partner goes to therapy and seems to deteriorate. As partners, you will be greatly alarmed if new behaviors surface that seem to suggest more pain. The reality is that therapy does not make someone feel better right away. As a matter of fact, therapy can initially allow feelings to surface that have not been visible before; it may give the person permission to think about past events previously ignored or avoided. It may take months before the person begins to feel some relief. It's important for you to know and remember that the expression of pent-up emotions is positive, and will have long-term positive impact.

Be consistent in your support and availability. Let your partner know that you are there if he or she needs to talk, wants your opinion, needs to be alone, or needs to be held. Let survivors know you are willing to do or say whatever is needed, and that you are receptive to hearing specifics. Be sure you assert that you don't feel put out, put upon, or burdened. Survivors are sensitive to asking for help from others and are afraid they don't deserve the attention or may ask too much.

It's Taking Too Long

Some partners have confided their impatience at how long the process of therapy may take. The length of treatment is highly individualized and there is **no set time** that can be guaranteed. Some therapy can take years, while other therapy can be brief. Yet another common form of therapy is continuous, with numerous breaks between periods of therapy.

It's important for you to recognize that therapy will take as long as it takes, and as long as your partner is interested in pursuing therapy, he or she must make that decision without outside pressure. If you feel that the therapy is too long, and is making the situation worse, ask your partner to let you know his or her feelings about therapy. Be careful not to sound impatient or communicate your frustrations to your partner. Instead, seek out others with whom you can share your feelings. If it is needed, seek out your own support system so your feelings are acknowledged and addressed without inadvertently pressuring your partner.

What's Going On?

Partners or friends may find themselves extremely curious about what's going on in the therapy. This is normal; you have probably encouraged your survivor friend or spouse to enter therapy and you may want to know the details. Remember that the therapy relationship is very personal and private; your partner will decide how much of the therapy process he or she tells you about. Be patient and let your partner or friend know that you are willing to listen **when and if** he or she may want to talk to you.

On occasion, your partner's therapist may ask you to come to one or more therapy sessions to help you better understand the process of therapy and recovery. This is done only with your partner's permission. If you find that your partner wants to explain certain concepts about therapy and yet he or she feels tongue-tied and wants you to talk directly with the therapist, approach the therapist with any questions or concerns you may have. Most therapists understand the importance of the significant relationships of their patients, and will likely be asking about them.

Can I Talk to the Therapist Directly?

The therapist cannot speak to you without your partner's permission. If you are interested in talking to your partner's therapist, and neither your partner nor the therapist has suggested this, approach your partner and be specific about why you would like to talk with the therapist. Use some of the communication principles presented in this book to approach your partner gently and directly about what you need. If your partner seems concerned or hesitant about the possibility, ask him or her to think it over and perhaps discuss it with the therapist. Be sure that you are ready to accept whatever decision your partner makes.

Why Can't My Partner Talk to Me?

The therapist–patient relationship is unique. One of the unique aspects of the therapy relationship is that no intimate relationship exists. The patient can talk freely without worrying about the therapist's feelings. It is sometimes easier to talk to someone who maintains emotional distance than to talk to an intimate friend or lover. For this reason, many people find it comfortable to talk to their therapist about subjects that may make them uncomfortable in other settings.

During the therapy relationship, your partner may develop more and more trust of the therapist. As trust grows, partners may find themselves turning to the therapist with their private thoughts and feelings. On occasion, they may seem more interested in discussing things with the therapist than with you. Some partners have told me that they feel "left out," somehow "replaced" by the therapist. You may find yourself having feelings of jealousy or resentment toward your partner's therapist. These are difficult emotions, and you must try to work on understanding them and working them through so they don't affect your support of the therapy process. Talking to others who have similar experiences can make you feel validated. You may also be able to share techniques for addressing your important feelings and thoughts. Your goal is to be helpful to your partner, and this is not always as simple as it sounds. You will likely experience a range of feelings, and you can't disregard them. Be sure you take as good care of yourself as you do of your partner.

My Partner's Becoming a Therapy Junkie!

Another issue can surface when your partner begins to get into other forms of therapy and seems to be spending a great deal of time away from home.

Some survivors will benefit not only from individual therapy but from group therapy, workshops for survivors, and self-help groups. In addition, many survivors find other programs helpful such as AA meetings, Al-Anon meetings, or ACOA (Adult Children of Alcoholics) meetings. Since these groups are available almost on a round-the-clock basis, you may miss your partner's company.

Remember that each survivor designs the recovery program that he or she needs. Also keep in mind that survivors may want to surround themselves with many support systems initially, and then select those programs that are found to be most beneficial. As recovery progresses, needs change. Be as supportive as possible, and if you find yourself alone

My partner's becoming a therapy junkie.

too much of the time, bring your feelings to the attention of your partner, and see if you can reach some kind of compromise. Your partner may be surprised to learn of your feelings, and may be quite willing to make some adjustments to the schedule.

Be sure you don't take your partner's active participation in the recovery process as a sign of personal rejection. Recovery requires a focus on self, and it will be more useful when it occurs within a supportive and understanding relationship. At the same time, your feelings are very important, and you need to give yourself as much kindness and support as possible.

Summary

Loving adult survivors of childhood abuse can present unique challenges and rewards. Survivors have had childhood experiences that create certain vulnerable areas, including feelings of shame, guilt, and self-deprecation; survivors frequently feel bad or unworthy. In addition, survivors commonly experience generalized fear and anxiety, bouts of depression, distrust, anger, or sexual problems. They may behave in ways that are not clearly explained or understood; they may find that current situations trigger sudden memories of the past.

Particularly because intimate relationships usually require trust, dependency, cooperation, and an equitable distribution of the balance of power, intimate relationships can cause the survivor to feel uncertainty and fear.

Survivors have a great deal of love to give and will be able to do so when they feel safety and consistency of care. Survivors have great capacity to receive and return affection once they learn to feel comfortable and confident.

In my experience the partners of adult survivors are compassionate and giving individuals, who are able to create safety and convey their feelings directly and clearly. It is only as a result of this communicated caring that the survivor can begin to feel optimistic about the future.

Partnerships based on honesty, love, and mutual respect

have great potential for growth and longevity. Together, the survivor and his or her partner can create a healthy and strong relationship with new memories and traditions, methods of celebration, and hopes and aspirations. Most importantly, partners learn from each other about how to communicate, resolve conflicts, and set and meet individual and collective goals.

The road is not without bumps. The road often has detours, and needs periodic maintenance work. But the road is not traveled alone, and companionship and support make the journey less stressful.

I wish you and your partner health and happiness in your futures. Please remember that in order for you to attend to your partner, you must also take care of yourself.

Resources for Survivors

Childhelp National Child Abuse Hotline
P.O. Box 630
Hollywood, CA 90028
(800) 422-4453

National Association for Children of Alcoholics (NACOA)
31706 Coast Highway, #201
So. Laguna, CA 92677
(714) 499-3889

National Self-Help Clearinghouse
City University of New York
33 W. 42nd Street, #1222
New York, NY 10036
(212) 840-1259

Survivors of Incest Anonymous
P.O. Box 21817
Baltimore, MD 21222
(301) 282-3400

Victims of Incest Can Emerge Survivors (VOICES)
P.O. Box 148309
Chicago, IL 60614
(312) 327-1500

Voices in Action
P.O. Box 148309
Chicago, IL 60614
(312) 327-1500

Suggested Readings

Bass, E., & Davis, L. (1988). *The Courage to Heal: A Guide for Women Survivors of Child Sexual Abuse.* New York: HarperCollins.

Bass, E., and Davis, L. (1983). *I Never Told Anyone.* New York: HarperCollins.

Bear, E., and Dimock, P. T. (1987). *Adults Molested as Children: A Survivors Manual for Women and Men.* Orwell, VT: Safer Society Press.

Biffle, C. (1989). *A Journey Through Your Childhood.* Los Angeles: Jeremy Tarcher.

Black, C. (1982). *It Will Never Happen to Me.* Denver, CO: Medical Administration Company.

Butler, S. (1978). *Conspiracy of Silence: The Trauma of Incest.* San Francisco: New Glide Publications.

Caruso, B. (1986). *Healing: A Handbook for Adult Victims of Sexual Abuse.* Minneapolis: Author.

Childhelp USA (1988). *Survivor's Guide.* Los Angeles Child Help Center, P.O. Box 630, Hollywood, CA 90028.

Daugherty, L. B. (1984). *Why Me? Help for Victims of Child Sexual Abuse (Even If They Are Adults Now).* Racine, WI: Mother Courage Press.

Davis, L. (1991). *Allies in Healing.* New York: Harper-Collins.

Davis, L. (1990). *The Courage to Heal Workbook*. New York: HarperCollins.

Donaforte, L. (1982). *I Remembered Myself: The Journal of a Survivor of Childhood Sexual Abuse*. Ukiah, CA.: Author.

Evert, K. (1987). *When You're Ready: A Woman's Healing from Childhood Physical and Sexual Abuse by Her Mother*. Rockville, MD: Launch Press.

Farmer, S. (1989). *Adult Children of Abusive Parents*. Los Angeles: Lowell House.

Gil, E. (1988). *Outgrowing the Pain: A Book for and About Adults Abused as Children*. New York: Dell Publishing.

Gil, E. (1990). *United We Stand: A Book for People with Multiple Personalities*. Rockville, MD: Launch Press.

Gravitz, H. L., and Bowden, J. D. (1985). *Recovery: A Book for Adult Children of Alcoholics*. Holmes Beach, FL: Learning Publications.

Helfer, R. E. (1978). *Childhood Comes First: A Crash Course in Childhood*. East Lansing, MI: Author.

Leehan, J., and Wilson, L. P. (1985). *Grown-up Abused Children*. Springfield, IL: Charles C Thomas.

Lew, M. (1990). *Victims No Longer: Men Recovering from Incest and Other Childhood Sexual Abuse*. New York: HarperCollins.

Maltz, W. (1991). *The Sexual Healing Journey: A Guide for Survivors of Sexual Abuse*. New York: HarperCollins.

McConnell, P. (1986). *A Workbook for Healing Adult Children of Alcoholics*. San Francisco: Harper San Francisco.

Miller, A. (1983). *For Your Own Good*. New York: Farrar, Straus & Giroux.

Miller, A. (1986). *Thou Shalt Not Be Aware: Psychoanalysis and Society's Betrayal of the Child*. New York: Meridan.

Montegna, D. (1989). *Prisoner of Innocence*. Rockville, MD: Launch Press.

Morris, M. (1982). *If I Should Die Before I Wake*. New York: J. P. Tarcher.

Rush, F. (1980). *The Best Kept Secret: Sexual Abuse of Children*. Englewood Cliffs, NJ: Prentice-Hall.

Sisk, S. L., and Hoffman, C. F. (1987). *Inside Scars*. Gainesville, FL: Pandora Press.

Thomas, T. (1989). *Men Surviving Incest: A Male Survivor Shares the Process of Recovery*. Rockville, MA: Launch Press.

Wilson, S. (1991). *Rising Above Shame: Healing Family Wounds to Self-Esteem*. Rockville, MD: Launch Press.

Wynne, C. E. (1981). *That Looks Like a Nice House*. Rockville, MD: Launch Press.